Liberal Education
and the
Modern
University

Liberal Education
and the
Modern
University

Charles Wegener

The
University
of
Chicago
Press

*Chicago and
London*

CHARLES WEGENER is the Howard L. Willett
Professor in the College and chairman of the
Committee on Ideas and Methods at the
University of Chicago.

The University of Chicago Press, Chicago 60637
The University of Chicago Press, Ltd., London

© 1978 by The University of Chicago
All rights reserved. Published 1978
Printed in the United States of America

82 81 80 79 78   5 4 3 2 1

Library of Congress Cataloging in Publication Data

Wegener, Charles.
   Liberal education and the modern university.

   Includes bibliographical references and index.
      1.   Education, Humanistic.   2.   Universities
and colleges—Curricula.   I.   Title.
LC1011.W43   378'.01'2   78–6789
ISBN: 0–226–87891–0

Contents

Preface

This book is not a treatise, a study, or a history. It is an attempt to rediscover and redefine a persistent problem in the interest of encouraging attempts at its solution. It advocates no particular solution, partly because, as it argues, any actual solution is a function not only of the various starting points of those who may attempt solutions but also of the particular circumstances in which they must rethink the problem and locate possibilities for attacking it. Fundamentally, I address myself to my fellow academics, on the assumption that the proximate source of educational innovation is to be found in educators. But I do not solely or even primarily address myself to those who study education—even higher education—but rather to all those who teach or influence teachers, and I am fully aware that professors are not the only sources of demands and proposals for educational change. Broadly then, I address myself to the academic world and those whom it serves, and I venture to hope that this inquiry may communicate to all of them some better idea of what is at stake in the conduct of the enterprise of education.

In other words, this is a "how-to-think-constructively-about" book. The history it contains is included in the interest of making an object for reflection the complex of institutional habits and aspirations which have formed our ideas about educational problems and within which we must begin any process of reconstruction. In fact, to a very large extent what is argued here is simply the product of reflection on the experience of education which I have been fortunate enough to acquire in a respectable number of years of teaching. Necessarily, therefore, I owe a literally incalculable debt to my own teachers and to my colleagues, among whom I must of course number students and many persons who may never have thought of themselves as teachers. In its final form it owes a special and immediate debt to Charles O'Connell and Karl Weintraub, whose readings of the manuscript produced a multitude of valuable corrections and suggestions, some of which, I fear, I did not adopt.

1

The Founders: Research

The institutional and intellectual situation in which we presently seek to formulate and solve the problems of liberal education is the product of a massive change which transformed American institutions of higher education in the latter years of the last century. For those who like significant moments, it is possible to advance February 22, 1876—the day on which Daniel Coit Gilman delivered his inaugural address as president of the newly opened Johns Hopkins University—as a plausible beginning, but whatever dating is selected, what is remarkable about the change is the rapidity with which it occurred and the extent of the transformation. Twenty-six years later, when Gilman retired from Johns Hopkins, President Harper of the University of Chicago summed up the transition as he saw it.

> We are celebrating in these days not only the twenty-fifth anniversary of the Johns Hopkins University . . . ; but we are celebrating likewise the close of the first period of university education in the United States.
> During this period the university idea has been introduced and established. Nor does the time within which this has taken place date far back. There were no universities in this country before the [Civil] war. There were, in fact, no large colleges. But within thirty years institutions have come into existence possessing, not only the name, but the character of universities; and old institutions have changed, not only their character, but their

1

names. In other words, the university idea has beyond question established itself upon a strong foundation.[1]

Perhaps a better choice of a date for the "close of the first period of university education in the United States"—one Harper might have chosen had he not been constrained by the occasion—would be February 1900, when the Association of American Universities, "composed of institutions on the North American Continent engaged in giving advanced or graduate instruction" and associated "for the purpose of considering matters of common interest relating to graduate study," was founded at a meeting summoned at the invitation of the presidents of Harvard, Columbia, Johns Hopkins, Chicago, and California. The original membership included nine other institutions: Michigan, Pennsylvania, Wisconsin, Catholic University, Clark, Cornell, Princeton, Stanford, and Yale. Significantly, the founding meeting was held at Chicago, and the first president of the association was "the representative of Harvard University."[2]

1. "The Contribution of Johns Hopkins, in William Rainey Harper, *The Trend in Higher Education* (Chicago: University of Chicago Press, 1905), p. 151. (The date on which this address was read is incorrectly given as February 22, 1903.)

2. Robert Hutchins was later to refer to the universities belonging to the AAU as "those which are willing to admit that they are the best." In their original description of themselves, they seem to be claiming to be the best *and only* universities—"on the North American Continent," that is (Association of American Universities, *Journal of Proceedings and Addresses of the First and Second Annual Conferences* [Chicago, 1901], pp. 7 *et seq*). According to Bernard Berelson (*Graduate Education in the United States* [New York: McGraw-Hill, 1960], p. 15) the five inviting institutions at that time conferred 55 percent of all "earned doctorates," and the other nine original members conferred another 33 percent. He does not say where the remaining 12 percent were earned. In 1948, by which time the association had thirty-four members (including two Canadian universities), the original constitution was amended so that the statement of purpose became "to consider and express opinions on matters of common interest relating to university policy," and the association came to describe itself as "composed of the North American continent the quality of whose graduate work in certain fields is high and, in addition, whose claims for inclusion are strong either because of the general standing of their programs or because of the high standing of one or more of their professional schools." Clearly these changes reflect changes of some importance in the world of universities. It is difficult not to have some nostalgic affection for the straightforward confidence of the original. (See *Journal of Proceedings and Addresses of the Forty-ninth Annual Conference* [Princeton, N.J., 1949], pp. 142–43, where the original and amended constitutions are printed side by side.)

It is difficult, one hundred years later, to convey the character of the transformation represented by what Harper called the "university idea." The institutional structures which emerged so rapidly in this period are, since they are basic to our own, those which we tend to assume as normal and therefore regard, unconsciously perhaps, as necessary and eternal. They have shaped us, and we find it difficult to imagine a world in which we could not have occurred. For academicians in particular they practically define patterns of work and career, and a different ordering of such functions, presupposed by a different set of social habits, is not easy to project. That these structures had to be *invented*—discovered and constructed—and that originally they were experiments in modes of organization of human energies the future and the consequences of which no one could fully foresee, may be as mysterious to us as any other act of creation. To ask whether, had we been "present at the creation," we would have ordered matters differently may be a meaningless question, since then "we" would have been somebody else; but it is not useless, as heirs and partially products of the tradition which was then founded, to endeavor to understand ourselves better by a reconstruction of the purposefulness realized in the transformation. We might then see our institutions not as inevitabilities but as agencies and products in a process in which purposes, variously and incompletely formulated, are variously and incompletely realized. We may also see *ourselves,* in significant respects, as possibilities admitting of practical alternatives rather than as eternal objects. Such an inquiry has, of course, the benefit of hindsight, but to the extent that we can imaginatively place ourselves at the beginning as well, hindsight will be modified by foresight: purpose by consequence and consequence by purpose. To know what we have been doing entails always the possibility, radical or modest, of significant redirection.

Harper spoke of the "university *idea*," but it was an idea which manifested itself in massive changes describable in almost physical terms. Whatever else it entailed, realizing the "idea" required the provision of facilities for intellectual and educational functions of a kind and on a scale previously unknown "on the North American continent." Speaking at the dedication of the library of Colorado College in 1894, Harper chose to discuss "the old and new in education" largely in terms of the provision of libraries and laboratories, emphasizing that both were practically new features of the academic world.

A quarter of a century ago the library in most of our institutions, even the oldest, was scarcely large enough, if one were to count the volumes, or valuable enough, if one were to estimate values, to deserve the name of library. So far as it had location, it was the place to which the professor was accustomed to make his way occasionally, the student almost never. It was open for consultation during perhaps one hour a day on three days a week. The better class of students, it was understood, had no time for reading. It was only the "ne'er do well," the man with little interest in the classroom textbook, who could find time for general reading. Such reading was a distraction, and a proposition that one might profit by consulting other books which bore upon the subject or subjects treated in the textbook would have been scouted. All such work was thought to be distracting. The addition of one hundred volumes in a year was something noteworthy. The place, seldom frequented, was some out-of-the-way room which could serve no other use. The librarian—there was none. Why should there have been? Any officer of the institution could perform the needed service without greatly increasing the burden of his official duties.[3]

Even in 1894 Harper must have thought this statement already incredible, for he goes on:

Is this statement overdrawn? Let me produce the evidence: The late librarian of Newberry Library, William Frederick Poole, to whom more than to any other belongs the credit of the existence of the new regime, so far as libraries are concerned, in an address delivered a few months before his death made this statement: "To those of us who graduated thirty, forty, or more years ago, books, outside of the textbooks used, had no part in our education. They were never quoted, recommended, nor mentioned by the instructors in the classroom. As I remember it, Yale College Library might as well have been in Weathersfield, or Bridgeport, as in New Haven, so far as the students in those days were concerned."[4]

3. "The Old and the New in Education," reprinted in Harper, *The Trend in Higher Education,* pp. 118–34.
4. Poole (1821–94) was before ending his career as first librarian of the Newberry Library successively librarian of the Mercantile Library Association of Boston, the Boston Athenaeum, the Cincinnati Public Library, and the Chicago Public Library. He was at Yale in 1842 and 1846–49. Harper quotes from *The University Library and the University Curriculum,* a Phi Beta Kappa Address delivered at Northwestern University in June 1893 (Chicago and New York: F. H. Revell Co., 1894). The passage quoted continues, "The college societies, however, supported and managed wholly by undergraduates, had good libraries, and here was where the students, and

But as Harper saw it the library, already "the center of the institutional activity," had an even more impressive future. "It will come to be, not simply a collecting agency, the house of storage, but also the agency for publication and distribution. . . . The publications of the future which are to exert the greatest influence for good upon mankind at large will be endowed publications. . . . The university press, therefore, is strictly a part of the university library, and through it, even in our day, we shall see the influence and power of the library greatly increased. That factor of our college and university work, the library, fifty years ago almost unknown, today already the center of the institution's intellectual activity, half a century hence—with its sister, the laboratory, almost equally unknown fifty years back—will, by absorbing all else, have become the institution itself."

The laboratory, that other pillar of "university work," was of equally recent origin. "Those of us who left college from twenty to twenty-five years ago scarcely knew such a thing as a laboratory. The library had a small place in college life; the laboratory had almost none." Charles William Eliot, who graduated from Harvard in 1853 at age nineteen, remembered that

> [i]n the Harvard College of my undergraduate days no laboratory instruction was given to the students; the sciences had to be learned from books and a few illustrated lectures. In my freshman year I became much interested in chemistry, and from the beginnings of my sophomore year I had the privilege of working in the small chemical laboratory which Josiah Parsons Cooke, instructor in chemistry, and soon (1851) to be appointed professor of chemistry, was allowed to fit up at his own expense in the basement of University Hall. During the last three years of

the professors besides, found their general reading. I was fortunate in being connected with one of those libraries, and here was where I began the study of bibliography; but never had the slightest assistance from any member of the faculty." In fact it was at Yale that he produced the first edition of what later came to be known as *Poole's Index to Periodical Literature*. Its original edition (1848) had an appropriately explicit title: *An Alphabetical Index to Subjects Treated in the Reviews and Other Periodicals to Which No Indexes Have Been Published*. This little book of 154 pages was the original of a bibliographical tool now, of course, taken to be indispensable. Subsequent editions and supplements (1853, 1882, five year supplements to 1906) of *Poole's Index* bore on their title page a motto supposedly composed by one of Poole's tutors at Yale "in honor of the index": *Qui scit ubi sit scientia habenti est proximus*, or, for a later age, "Who knows where knowledge is has it within his grasp."

my college course I did much work in that little laboratory every
week. . . . To the best of my knowledge and belief I was the
only undergraduate in Harvard College who had the privilege
of studying a science by the laboratory method.[5]

Nor should it be inferred from Eliot's language that graduate students were more privileged. The Graduate School of Arts and
Sciences became fully established only in 1890, during Eliot's own
presidency. It is true that the Lawrence Scientific School had been
established in 1848, but as late as 1856 the provision of laboratories
for chemical instruction was still almost inconceivable. Eliot, then
a tutor in mathematics, found himself engaged in teaching chemistry
in the medical school by a somewhat remarkable sequence of
events.

I happened to make the acquaintance of the Medical School as
early as 1856. In October of that year Professor Josiah P.
Cooke, who had for several years given the course of lectures on chemistry to medical students, as well as all the instruction in chemistry
which undergraduates in Harvard College then received, and had
equipped his laboratories at both places at his own expense or
his father's, got into a lively altercation with the Medical Faculty
about their practice of giving the degree of M.D. on slight oral
examinations to any candidate who passed in five subjects out of
nine. At the end of the altercation Professor Cooke resigned his
place in the Medical Faculty, told them he should not lecture
again in the School, ripped out of his laboratory at the School
the furnaces and other fixtures he had put in there, and carted
them and all the rest of the equipment out to Cambridge. The
Medical session was to open in a few days. The Faculty sent a
protest to the Corporation; and the Corporation suggested to
Professor Cooke that he give, or provide for, the course in
chemistry at the Medical School which had been announced for
the session of 1856–57. Professor Cooke felt on reflection that he
had been somewhat precipitate; so he accepted the suggestion of
the Corporation. . . . When I became a tutor in mathematics in
1854, I went on with my chemical studies under Professor Cooke;
and in 1856 was carrying on some chemical researches in his
laboratory and under his guidance. Accordingly, when he asked
me to give the course in the Medical School for him, saying
that he would send in from Cambridge all the laboratory furniture
I should need and all the chemical apparatus which would be

5. Charles William Eliot, *A Late Harvest: Miscellaneous Papers Written
between Eighty and Ninety* (Boston: Atlantic Monthly Press, 1924), p. 9.

needed to illustrate my lecture, I had to do what he wished me to.[6]

Harper, in "The Old and New in Education," no doubt simplifies greatly a complex history, but the need for libraries and laboratories bulked large in the minds of those who, like him, were engaged in the realization of the university idea. Gilman's inaugural address gave notable stress to the need for such facilities.

What will the buildings be?

At first, temporary, but commodious; in the heart of the city, accessible to all; fitted for lectures, laboratories, library and collections. At length, permanent, on the site at Clifton,[7] not a medieval pile, I hope, but a series of modern institutions; not a monumental, but a serviceable, group of structures. At present laboratories are demanded on a scale and in a variety hitherto unknown, for chemistry, physics, geology and mineralogy, comparative anatomy, physiology, pathology.[8]

And it is probably worthy of note that in citing examples of what was wanted he mentioned European institutions only. "Oxford with its New Museum; Cambridge, with its Cavendish Laboratory; Owens College, with its excellent workrooms; South Kensington, with the new apartments of Huxley and Frankland; Leipsic, Vienna, Berlin, all afford illustrations of the kind of structures we shall need."

Museums were also part of the equipment envisaged as necessary to carry on university work. At Chicago, from the founding of the university, there existed a "Board of Libraries, Laboratories, and Museums," and by the end of the university's first decade in 1902 it presided over an extensive establishment. The libraries in-

6. Ibid., pp. 33–34.

7. Clifton was a more than three-hundred acre estate (then outside the city limits of Baltimore) which Johns Hopkins bequeathed to the University and which he hoped would eventually be its site. This dream was never realized. Whittled down to some 250 acres by condemnation proceedings on the part of the municipal water board and the Baltimore and Ohio Railroad, Clifton was eventually sold in 1895 to the city of Baltimore for a public park. The financial history of Johns Hopkins is complex. There was an acute crisis in 1887, when the university's endowment income was reduced by about three-fourths as a result of a suspension of dividends on common stock by the Baltimore and Ohio Railroad.

8. Reprinted in Daniel C. Gilman, *University Problems in the United States* (New York: Century Co., 1898). The quotations are to be found on p. 31.

cluded 354,592 volumes, and the university's buildings included
Kent Chemical Laboratory, Ryerson Physical Laboratory, Walker
Museum (containing "collections in Anthropology, Geology, Geography, Mineralogy, Petrography and historical Paleontology"),
Haskell Oriental Museum, Hull Biological Laboratories (four
buildings), and Yerkes Observatory. These buildings represented
more than half of the money expended for buildings in the first
decade of the university's life.[9]

Harper was aware that physical facilities by themselves guaranteed nothing, but he refused to apologize for dealing only with
externals.

> I have spoken of the libraries and the laboratories with their
> equipment as constituting the outside of educational work. This,
> however, is only partly true. When we realize that the method
> and spirit of the work are largely determined by these outside
> factors, we may consent to allow them a place on the inside. The
> character of the work fifty years ago was determined in large
> measure by their absence; their presence has transformed the
> whole work of education, and the work of transformation will
> continue, for our children will see realized what we today would
> not even dare to dream of. Nor must it be supposed that this work
> will affect only the methods of teaching and of study. This change
> has already taken place; for in every subject of the college cur-
> riculum the laboratory method and the library method now hold
> full sway.[10]

The language in which leaders like Gilman and Harper discussed
the inside of university work may strike us as odd, partly because
they use one term, "science," more generally than we now tend to
do and partly because what is for us a word and an idea so common

---

9. *The President's Report, July, 1892–July, 1902* (Chicago: University of
Chicago Press, 1903), p. cxxiv. Harper gives the sum as $1,161,816, a figure
not including Haskell, but he was eager for more: "No need of the University
is greater today than that of the central Library. . . . Large sums of money
are needed for the purchase of books for the various Departments"; and he
listed at least four more laboratories which were needed. As for museums:
"our faculties are strongly manned; the buildings are large and beautiful and
numerous; the libraries are only half way developed; the museums have
hardly begun. It is in respect to the libraries and museums that the greatest
effort should be made in these coming years" (ibid., pp. cxxv–cxxvii). It was
not to be so, at least not so far as museums were concerned.

10. "The Old and New in Education," in *The Trend in Higher Education*
(Chicago, 1905), p. 133.

as to be accepted almost without thought was for them something of a novelty—"research," or, as Harper tended to prefer, "investigation." In June 1903, after his retirement as president of Johns Hopkins and his assumption of the presidency of the Carnegie Institution of Washington, Gilman journeyed to Chicago to address the university's forty-seventh convocation.[11] When he reprinted his address in 1906 in *The Launching of a University and Other Papers,* he entitled it simply "Research: A Speech delivered at the Convocation of the University of Chicago, June, 1903."[12] In the program of the convocation and as reprinted in the *University of Chicago Record,* it bore the title "Prospects of Science in the United States at the Beginning of the Twentieth Century." What he had to say is worth quoting at some length. After disclaiming, before "an audience which includes many eminent specialists, . . . expertness in any branch," he did claim to be an "observer of the progress of science, who has had opportunities, prolonged and in some respects, unique, for watching, and now and then for helping, the workers."

Observation from this watchtower will be clearer after some of the underbrush which might interrupt our vision has been removed. I begin by reminding you that during the last century the range of science was vastly extended. Its domain is now imperial. When some of us were undergraduates science was restricted to the phenomena of the visible world, to the study of those objects which might be measured by instruments of precision. Chemistry, physics, and natural history (to which geology, on the one hand, and medicine, on the other, were related) were the chief departments.[13] Mathematics, pure and applied, was an

11. At this same convocation an honorary degree was conferred on Nicholas Murray Butler, who had become president of Columbia the previous year.
12. Daniel C. Gilman, *The Launching of a University and Other Papers* (New York: Dodd Mead & Co., 1906). The quotations which follow are to be found on pages 238–39 and 242–43.
13. It is probably not superfluous to remark that the word "department," used very frequently in these years, was also in a state of transition. It did not yet mean, in the academic world, primarily and almost exclusively an institutional arrangement or subdivision. Rather it still meant—or could be alternately used to mean—a branch of knowledge or a subject matter which might or might not be institutionally separated or represented. There was, therefore, a far clearer recognition in those days that there might be, within a department in the institutional sense, many departments of knowledge or study. Harper, for example, frequently tended to talk as if the institutional arrangements were a matter of convenience for the investigators, largely

entity apart. Now all these subjects are subjected to manifold subdivisions, as branches of science; at the same time, a host of younger aspirants claim recognition as belonging to the parent stem. History, archaeology, geography, meteorology, agriculture, philology, psychology, logic, sociology, and even jurisprudence and theology, are employing the scientific method, with increasing success, and demand recognition in the surrogate's court, as the next of kin.

He went on to speculations in intellectual history and intellectual organization, but after considering the conditions favorable to the advancement of science in the United States (among them, "the admission of educated women—not in exceptional cases, but in considerable and increasing numbers—to the opportunities for original investigation"), he pointed to the consequences.

Under these conditions a new term has become current in our academic vocabulary, the term "research." It is a new term, not a new idea, for Herodotus and Aristotle, Roger Bacon and Francis Bacon, Isaac Newton and Linnaeus, Franklin and Rumford, and hosts of American forerunners and contemporaries, eager in the pursuit of knowledge, have made contributions to the storehouses of mankind which still furnish seed-corn to the cultivators and experience to experimenters. "Research" is not a felicitous term. Neither, for that matter, is the term "university," which originally meant the entire body, or corporation, of civic, ecclesiastical, or educational authorities. Centuries ago the world gave its preference to "university" and turned a cold shoulder upon *studium generale*. Apparently, "research" has likewise come to stay.

The word was presented to the English-speaking world in 1875 in a volume entitled *The Endowment of Research,* by Dr. Appleton, an English Scholar. We have the authority of his learned

---

because he saw those institutional arrangements as serving the more basic functions represented by the departments in which investigators carried on their work, so that the institutional question was what "departments" could usefully be grouped together in a "department."

An interesting example of the older use of this word occurs in the memoirs of John W. Burgess, founder of the School of Political Science at Columbia. Speaking of Amherst in 1864–67 he says: "There was not much natural science. . . . Only the departments of chemistry and mineralogy were represented, the first by Professor William S. Clark, and the second by Professor Charles U. Shepard" (*Reminiscences of an American Scholar: The Beginnings of Columbia University* [New York: Columbia University Press, 1934], p. 50).

associate, the humanist Mark Pattison, for saying that it was then
a new conception made popular under the term "research." "The
term," he remarks, "is inappropriate enough, but, like all complex conceptions, no one word in the language is anything like
adequate to cover this conception; yet some one word must be
employed when we wish to speak much of the thing." Whatever
results may have followed in England, the arguments of Pattison
and Appleton and their associates had a very strong influence
upon the organization of one American university in the year
1876, and since that time the conception of "research" has spread
throughout our land from peak to peak like the signal fires described by the Greek dramatists.

I wish it were possible even now to use the words "investiga-
tion" and "investigators," but certainly something more than an
act of the legislature will be required before the child can throw
off the name by which it has been christened. Even that suggested
is not very good. The "advancement of knowledge" was Lord
Bacon's phrase, adopted by the founder of the Smithsonian
Institution for the "advancement and diffusion of knowledge."
"Creative action," says President Eliot, was the phrase of Ralph
Waldo Emerson. "Constructive scholarship" is proposed by
Münsterberg.[14]

14. One hardly knows where to begin in annotating these excerpts. To
the use of the term "science" we shall return, but Gilman's remarks about
"research" require some correcting at this point. *The Endowment of Research* was actually entitled *Essays on the Endowment of Research by Various
Writers* and was published in 1876, not 1875. The "various writers" included
Mark Pattison, R. L. Nettleship, and Dr. Appleton, that is, Charles Edward
Cutts Birch Appleton, perhaps better known as the founder and, until his
death, editor of *The Academy,* one of the original purposes of which was to
serve as an organ of those who hoped to achieve such reform of Oxford
and Cambridge as would give a proper place to research. The date of publication of *Essays on the Endowment of Research* is significant: it is part of the
discussion which reached a more formal stage in passage of the Act of 1877,
which established a commission of reform for Oxford. Max Müller reviewed
the *Essays* in *The Academy* (May 13, 1876), describing the "advocates of
the Endowment of Research" as "those who wish to make Oxford not only
a place of teaching, but a place of learning." The terms in which he discussed the problem suggest the extent to which the same directions of change
in university work were being sensed and advocated in England. It seemed
obvious to him that "a better library, a larger museum, a more central
botanic garden, more lecture-rooms and laboratories" should enjoy priority
over the system of fellowships which bestowed "liberal rewards on young
men who have just finished their academic career, and many of whom will
never render any service whatever to the university. Or if it be asked whether
it would be more beneficial to the university to endow a professor of English

Whatever else the university idea and university work were (and
are), "research," "the advancement of knowledge," or "investigation" were clearly essential. It was a complex (perhaps even a con-

---

literature and of many other branches of learning not yet represented at
Oxford, or to send checks for 300 £ to fifty young men scattered over England and the Continent, the answer again would be hardly doubtful." What
was not so clear to him was "how young men could best be encouraged to
devote themselves to what is called Independent Research. The fact cannot
be denied, and these Essays supply ample proof of it, that England does not
hold the place she ought to hold among the principal nations who supply the
intellectual market of the world. It is easy . . . to cite a number of distinguished
men who have been educated at Oxford and Cambridge. England will never
be without men of genius. But England is deficient in those men who add atom
to atom, who write short articles full of new facts, who publish in a 'programme' the results of years of labour, who watch the spots on the sun
until they reduce them to a system, who collate MSS., who make indices,
who are great in those little things without which there is no real greatness to
be achieved in science or scholarship. Science does not grow rapidly; it grows
slowly, and its real advance is marked by small 'monographies' [*sic*] far
more than by big books. . . . The majority of undergraduates may be satisfied
if they carry away from the university that amount of general culture which
is essential to a gentleman; but we want at least a small minority of workers
who should improve and increase the stock of human knowledge, who should
devote themselves to special lines of study, and should take care that the
intellectual exports of England should never fall below the intellectual im-
ports."

Mark Pattison (rector of Lincoln, 1861–84), once thought to be the model
for Mr. Casaubon in *Middlemarch,* was a central figure in the Oxford reform
movement. His *Suggestions on Academical Organization* (1868) proposed,
in effect, to abolish the traditional colleges and fellowships and substitute an
organization of nine faculties constituted by a "professoriate." According to
John Sparrow, Pattison's essay in *Essays on the Endowment of Research*
"reminded Lord Salisbury's Commission . . . that, though their task osten-
sibly dealt only with finance, it concerned the fundamental purpose of the
University. They would be dealing with large revenues, at present deployed
in providing prize fellowships for sinecurists; were those revenues to be
transferred to tutors, who—with or without the title of professor—would
spend their time preparing students for examinations, or were they to endow
a real professoriate, in which the occupant of every Chair was 'the master of
his science and its representative before the world'?" (John Sparrow, *Mark
Pattison and the Idea of a University* [London: Cambridge University Press,
1967], p. 124.)

Gilman's citation of Bacon is curiously inaccurate. Presumably he means
to refer to the work entitled (in its English version) *Of the Proficience and
Advancement of Learning.* The Latin version is entitled *De dignitate et aug-
mentis scientiarum.* I have not been able to locate Eliot's reference to Emerson.

fused) idea, but it had massive practical implications. In the working out of these consequences the idea itself took on a content, a substantiality, which, as Harper and Gilman saw, made it almost palpable. Briefly, the idea and the work it demanded amounted to a revolution in institutional structure, in professional function, and in curricular and educational content and activity. It remolded the actuality of an institution of learning and education; it gave new meaning to the "professoriate"; it removed the limitations on subjects and subject matters which had characterized schools, colleges, and universities; and, inevitably, it imposed new requirements, new activities, new options, and new problems upon students—that is, it effectively redefined teaching and learning.

We have already noted the massive reorganization of facilities—what Harper aptly called the "outside" of "university work"—which this revolution required. But the expansion of facilities—libraries, laboratories, and museums and their lineal descendents in the form of computers, cyclotrons, and Moog synthesisers—brought in its train a variety of other functionaries who became indispensable parts of the educational system. Librarians, laboratory technicians, curatorial staffs, and research assistants represented a new set of members of the institution. No longer was a college or an educational institution definable as students and teachers in some sort of minimal physical facility with an occasional book. Garfield's famous remark about Mark Hopkins, a log, and a student was probably already conservative in 1871, when it was made. Thirty years later it would have to be understood as an exercise in nostalgia. Students were differentiated into new groups: the graduate students, who fully participated in university work and themselves became apprentices and assistants in investigation, and the undergraduates, who were frequently thought to be dispensable. There was also a distinction developing between the graduate student who sought merely to participate in research and the graduate student who sought professional qualification in law, medicine, divinity, or technology.[15]

15. Part of the effort was to make professional schools truly graduate schools. As late as 1909 much remained to be accomplished in this respect. The Association of American Universities, at its meeting in that year, received a report of the Special Committee on Aim and Scope of the Association which in part addressed itself to the question how a university should be defined. One of the questions had to do with whether institutions had professional schools, admission to which required at least two years of col-

The academic staff, which had once consisted of the professors of the various subjects which constituted the curriculum, was now —generally following the German university model—organized into faculties which in turn were subdivided into departments. Very rapidly the problems inherent in such an organization became evident, and it is probably significant that they tended to be stated in relation to the work of students. Recurrently, in the early years of the University of Chicago, Harper pointed to the developing problems. As early as 1896 he said

> Another topic to which I desire to call the attention of my colleagues, not as individuals, but as faculties, is that of the correlation of the student's work. The different departments are organized as departments for the convenience of administration. It is impossible in most instances to draw a sharp line of separation. . . . Over against the tendency to separate departments farther and farther from each other, the movement should be encouraged to bring the departments more closely together. The work of the student in the future will not be cut off into departments; on the contrary, it will be the study of problems which will lead him into and through many departments of study. The need for correlation does not receive from most of us the appreciation which it deserves.[16]

Nor was the statement—perhaps somewhat startling to the modern academic ear—that the organization into departments was a matter

---

lege work. The following sentences are revealing: "Your committee reports that the University of Iowa, the University of Kansas, and the University of Nebraska appear to be eligible for membership, because each of these universities possesses a creditable graduate school and each has announced that two years of college work are to be required for admission to its medical department. . . . [T]he University of Indiana is eligible for membership, because this university possesses a creditable graduate school and has definitely fixed and announced a requirement of two years of college work for admission to candidacy for a degree in law." (Association of American Universities, *Journal of Proceedings and Addresses of the Tenth Annual Conference* [Chicago, 1909], Appendix II, p. 65). See also the paper, delivered at this same meeting, titled "The College in the University," and particularly the discussion which follows, in which President Eliot took the position that the practice of accepting the first year of work in a professional school as a basis for awarding a bachelor's degree "means the sacrifice of the last fourth of the American college outright." Yet he did not know of any institution "having both college and university professional schools, except Harvard, which absolutely refuses to adopt it" (ibid., p. 41).

16. "Sixteenth Quarterly Statement of the President," *University of Chicago Record* 1, no. 28 (1896): 384.

of "convenience" unconsidered. Two years later his words seem to express some exasperation:

> An arrangement of work which is formal and which has been introduced merely for the sake of convenience[17] must not be permitted to interfere with the best interests of students or of instructors or of the University at large. In our own University this evil seems to be greatest in the departments of science.[18]

The model of the new university contained more, however, than graduate faculties, undergraduate faculties, and departments. Inherent in it also, for reasons which we shall come to examine, was the notion of professional schools. There is a well-established myth at the University of Chicago that Harper did not approve of engineering schools or schools of music and art. In fact, he fully shared the general assumption of his fellow-founders that the university and university work must be extended to encompass not only the established professional faculties of law, medicine, and divinity but a whole series of others. His original plan for the university, published before it opened its doors, provided for an organization of the work of the university into the university proper, the university extension work, and the university publication work. The university proper consisted of academies, colleges, affiliated colleges, and schools. Of the schools he said:

> Of these there will be organized—
>
> (1) The Graduate School, which will include all graduate work of a non-professional character.
>
> (2) The Divinity School, which will include the curriculum of study ordinarily presented by Divinity Schools.
>
> As soon as the funds of the University permit there will also be established—
>
> (3) The Law School.

17. It seems clear that part of what Harper meant by "convenience of administration" was the device he employed in constructing his faculties. Briefly, his technique was to appoint a "Head Professor" who then constructed a department. The dangers and effectiveness of this mode of working are discussed with candor and shrewdness in his decennial report (*The President's Report, July 1892–July, 1902*, pp. xviii–xix). But he clearly also meant that any such division was a matter of convenience because no serious intellectual enterprise could be conducted in isolation. His favorite way of making this point was to say, in one form or another, that "the lines of department organization may not be strictly drawn" (Ibid., p. xx).

18. "Twenty-fifth Quarterly Statement of the President," *University of Chicago Record* 3, no. 32 (1898): 199–200.

(4) The Medical School.

(5) The School of Engineering, which will include Civil, Mechanical, and Electrical Engineering.

(6) The School of Pedagogy.

(7) The School of Fine Art.

(8) The School of Music.[19]

That all of these ambitions were not fulfilled does not make them less a part of the idea of a university as Harper and his fellow founders saw it. The most successful model for this effort was undoubtedly the Johns Hopkins University Medical School. In his will, Johns Hopkins had provided for a hospital which he intended should "ultimately form a part of the Medical School of that University for which I have made ample provision."[20] Gilman's inaugural was addressed at length to the desirability of the early establishment of the school, but it was in fact not until 1893 that it opened its doors, in conjunction with the hospital. Abraham Flexner, who probably exerted as much influence as any one man on the development of American medical education, was to say in 1946 about the university and the medical school:

> Thus at precisely the right moment, the University had set up a new pattern, meeting the country's need, and this pattern was copied by other academic institutions as rapidly as personnel was available and funds obtainable. In the same way, the Trustees of the Hospital, at precisely the right moment and under precisely the same kind of leadership, set up a new pattern in medical education and in hospital-university relationship that has within fifty years become the ideal which medical schools and teaching hospitals throughout the country have striven to attain.[21]

Charles W. Eliot, speaking in 1897 at the dedication of Columbia's new campus on Morningside, found it clear that the American universities would, "like Columbia, maintain at large centers of population well-equipped schools for all the learned and scientific professions."[22]

Integral to and consequent upon these institutional reorientations was a redefinition of the professional function of the aca-

19. *The President's Report, July 1892–July, 1902,* pp. 511 *et seq.*

20. Abraham Flexner, *Daniel Coit Gilman, Creator of the American Type of University* (New York: Harcourt, Brace and Co., 1946), p. 110.

21. Ibid., p. 111.

22. Charles W. Eliot, *Educational Reform: Essays and Addresses* (New York: Century Co., 1898), p. 398.

demic. The new professor was to be first and foremost an investigator. The way in which these purposes flowed together is lucidly set forth in an account of Gilman's statement to the Hopkins trustees concerning his plans for the university whose president he might become.

> He said . . . in substance, that he would make it the means of promoting scholarship of the first order, and this by only offering the kind of instruction to advanced students which other universities offer in their post-graduate courses, and leaving the kind of work done by undergraduates to be done elsewhere. For this purpose he would select as professors men now standing in the front rank in their own fields; he would pay them well enough to leave them at their ease as regards the commoner and coarser cares; would give them only students who were far enough advanced to keep them constantly stimulated to the highest point; and he would exact from them yearly proof of the diligent and fruitful cultivation of their specialties by compelling them to print somewhere the results of their researches. Now what this means . . . may be inferred when we say that we could at this moment name twenty men, employed at small salaries in existing colleges, whose work in certain fields of research would be of inestimable value to the science and literatures of the world, but who are compelled, in order to earn their livelihood, to pass most of their time teaching the rudiments to boys, or preparing school-books; and that American graduates who would like to pursue certain lines of culture to their latest limits are compelled to go abroad or content themselves with the necessarily imperfect aid which they can get in the post-graduate courses from overworked and half-paid professors who are doing the duty of schoolmasters.[23]

The elements of national pride, of contempt for the drudgery of schoolmastering, and the sense of the dignity and (quite literally) worth of the new professoriate and its productions are here nicely compounded.

From the beginning, in fact, it was not always clear why there needed to be students at all, or put the other way around, why there was any intrinsic connection between investigation and education or teaching—publication, of course, but why not a purely research professoriate? The founders tended to be somewhat unclear on this point. Sometimes they spoke as if only financial limitations

23. *Nation* January 28, 1875. Quoted in Flexner, *Daniel Coit Gilman,* p. 50.

made such positions impossible, desirable as they might be; though sometimes they waived the question of desirability until it could be a practical one. But they had no doubt about the priorities involved. A typical statement by Harper, made in a moment of some financial stringency, strikes the balance and reveals the stresses in a characteristically strenuous way.

Much has been said of the importance of investigation on the part of the University instructor. It is an opportune moment to lay emphasis upon the work of teaching as distinguished from that of investigating. There is danger that the importance of teaching may be overlooked. The young doctor sometimes forgets that the institution in which he works is under obligation to furnish the best possible instruction to the students whom it has gathered within its walls. For him to teach is a burdensome task. He would spend all his time in investigation. In view of what I have said on other occasions in reference to the duty of university men to investigate, I may not be charged with failure to appreciate the importance of this function. If an institution has funds with which to support men whose whole time may be given to investigation, nothing more in such cases should be expected. In our own institution we have not reached this ideal point of development. A certain amount of teaching, according to the statutes, is required of every officer. If a man is unable to teach, he cannot rightly receive an appointment in the University. If, after having been appointed, he shows inability to teach, The University, in justice to its students, must without question find someone to take his place who is able to teach. It is a criminal act on the part of an institution to retain as teacher a man who cannot teach. I wish to call the attention of my colleagues to this matter and to ask the question whether in any case energy and strength which belong by right to students of the University have been wrongly employed in investigation.[24]

24. "Sixteenth Quarterly Statement of the President," *University of Chicago Record* 1, no. 28 (1896): 383–84. In his decennial report Harper was clearer about research professorships, but it will be noted that his statement is a guarded one: "There should be established Research Professorships, the occupants of which might lecture or not according to the best interests of the work in which they are engaged. This is practically the character of the Professorships in the [Yerkes] Observatory. There should be chairs in other Departments, perhaps a chair in every Department, to which there might be made a permanent appointment, or which might be occupied for a longer or a shorter period by the various members of the Department capable of doing research work" *The President's Report, July 1892–1902,* p. xxv.

Even when the priority does not seem so clear, the result is much the same. Eliot argued that research was an indispensable function in a university partly because "a university which is not a place of research will not long continue to be a good place of teaching."[25] Gilman thought that the university function of distributing knowledge entailed teaching:

> The scholar does but half his duty who simply acquires knowledge. He must share his possessions with others. This is done, in the first place, by the instruction of pupils. Experience has certainly demonstrated that, with rare exceptions, those men are most learned who produce most. The process of acquiring seems to be promoted by that of imparting. The investigator who is surrounded by a bright circle of friendly inquisitors and critics finds his best powers developed by this influence.[26]

It is difficult, in retrospect, not to hear in all such pronouncements a certain amount of confusion (did students exist for the stimulation of investigators or . . . ?) and perhaps ultimately a note of wishful thinking.[27]

25. Eliot, *Educational Reform*, p. 231.

26. Gilman, "Utility of Universities," in *University Problems in the United States*, pp. 57–58. But see again the 1903 convocation address at the University of Chicago. Speaking then of the founder of the corporation of which he had just become the head, he said: "Mr. Carnegie had the sagacity to perceive that education and investigation are distinct functions of civilized life; and that they may be promoted by different corporations. He differentiated the two chief objects of a university—instruction and research. He did not intimate that these two functions must always be separated. Nobody thinks so. They may be united." (Gilman, *The Launching of a University* [New York, 1906], p. 250; see also pp. 243–44, where Gilman seems to want to confine the term "professor" to the investigator who also teaches, while recognizing that some of the most distinguished "have done their best work without pedagogical obligations.")

27. The question received a thorough airing at the seventh annual conference of the Association of American Universities (March 1906). Papers on the question "To What Extent Should the University Investigator be Relieved from Teaching?" by the presidents of Stanford and Yale, David Starr Jordan and Arthur T. Hadley, were the basis for the discussion. Both papers, particularly Jordan's, are well worth reading. At this distance what seems striking is the realistic attitude of all the participants toward research (they were sceptical of the value of much of it), their insistence that the separation of research (or investigation) and teaching was a generally dangerous idea, and their reiterated appreciation of the manifold forms and possible interrelations of both of the activities they were attempting to characterize. William James was present as the representative of Harvard and makes a very

Implicit in this conception of the professorial function insofar as it involved or required teaching were assumptions as to the nature of the teaching activity itself. The investigator surrounded by his "bright circle of friendly inquisitors and critics" is an image of the seminar—the sharing of work in progress by master and apprentices in the work, an image far different from that of the schoolmaster leading his pupils through recitations of textbook formulae. The other professorial forum—apart from publication, of course—was the lecture, but the lecture in which he reported the results of his own research in something like the form in which he wished to give them to the world. Again the model was certainly in large part the German professor. John Burgess, founder of the first graduate faculty at Columbia,[28] described in his memoirs the impression made on him by the habits of the German universities in the early 1870s. At Leipzig, in 1872, he "inscribed [himself] for the lectures of Windscheid, Roscher, Voigt, and Wuttke." In Voigt's lecture room he witnessed an extraordinary and revealing scene.

> It was the custom of the old King of Saxony, Johann, to visit his university annually and to hear a lecture from each of the chief professors. He came in my sojourn at Leipzig and attended a lecture by Professor Voigt. The subject of the lecture was Julius Caesar, whom Voigt described as a cold, calculating, untrustworthy Machiavellian character. At the close of the lecture the king rose up and said: "Mr. Professor, I did not know that Julius was so cold and calculating a nature. Just remember his tender relations to Cleopatra." Voigt did not catch, on account of his impaired hearing, what the king was saying. The students, however, understood His Majesty's words perfectly and began scraping their feet on the floor, laughing, and cheering. This greatly disturbed Voigt, but he did not know what to say, being entirely

---

characteristic interjection into the edited transcript of the discussion of the papers. (Association of American Universities, *Journal of Proceedings and Addresses of the Seventh Annual Conference* [Chicago, 1906]. pp. 23–51.)

28. The School of Political Science was founded in 1880. That Burgess and his colleagues saw quite clearly that Columbia College thus committed itself to becoming a university is apparent in his account of the cablegram he received in Paris in June 1880. "I was awakened by a loud knock on the door of my sleeping room about five o'clock. On going to the door, an American cablegram was handed me. It read: 'Thank God, the university is born. Go ahead.' It was signed 'Samuel B. Ruggles.' This meant that the trustees of Columbia College had, on the day before, adopted the plan for founding the School of Political Science." (Burgess, *Reminiscences,* pp. 194–95.) Columbia did not designate itself a university until 1896.

ignorant of what it was all about. The king, however, now spoke again and in somewhat louder tones. He said: "Professor, do you follow Mommsen in your study of Roman history?" The professor heard the shorter sentence and colored to the very roots of his hair, for it contained an implication which any German professor would regard as an affront if spoken by anyone short of majesty. In a proud and dignified tone Voigt replied: "No, Your Majesty, I make my own investigations."[29]

Clearly the royal sensitivity to the tenderness of Julius was not matched by an equal concern for the professor's tenderness to the suggestion that his professorial and lectorial function could be discharged in "following" anything or anyone other than his own "investigations." Was he not, in the words of Mark Pattison, supposedly "the master of his science and its representative before the world"?

Burgess's account of the pedagogy employed in the graduate School of Political Science is not only lucidly informative but exemplifies the conscious employment of European precedents and an equally conscious adaptation to American conditions.

> Our method of instruction was by lecture, reference reading, examinations every few days on the lectures and the references, and research work in the seminar conducted by each professor. We had as models of university teaching the methods of the German universities, of the Sorbonne and the Collège de France, and the École libre des sciences politiques. We did not follow them implicitly, but tried to combine the excellences, as we considered them, of all and eschew the defects. We were conscious from considerable and wide experience that American students were neither Germans nor Frenchmen, and we endeavoured to make our school an American School adapted to the higher instruction of American students. It was for this reason that we insisted upon more frequent examinations upon the lectures and reference readings and a more special oversight of the work of each student. We had felt quite decidedly that the lack of close control and acquaintance between teacher and pupil was a serious defect in the foreign school. We had discovered that, while the more brilliant minds among the students were able to surmount this defect, the average man suffered from it. We felt that the European system produced a splendid aristocracy of scholars, but we also felt it our duty to do something for democracy, even in letters and science.

29. Ibid., pp. 108–9.

We had not been able to learn much from the English model. At that time the so-called English university was a number of undergraduate colleges grouped together in one place. They did nothing for graduate or university work, except in the way of fellowships conferred after graduation upon students who had been successful in undergraduate work. These men lived in the dormitories, as we call them, of the different colleges, on the fellowship stipends, and educated themselves by reading in the libraries and by social intercourse with the men more advanced then they in the different branches of knowledge. They were not, however, brought under any regular faculty instruction.[30]

Finally, the university idea and university work transformed the curricular structure of American education not only by adding graduate schools and turning professional schools into graduate schools but, by consequence, profoundly altering the courses of study in colleges and preparatory schools as well. It would be as easy to say, in hindsight, that the traditional structures were destroyed, but at the time what was more apparent was the expansion of possibilities and the liberation inherent in the removal of limitations.[31] Universities took all knowledge for their province—in principle. It was always recognized that one could not do everything, but it seemed that it was only a matter of resources and, significantly, circumstantially determined needs. Gilman's inaugural rehearses the agreed-upon commonplaces:

1. All sciences are worthy of promotion; or, in other words, it is useless to dispute whether literature or science should receive more attention. . . .

30. Ibid., pp. 198–99. Burgess's account of what happened to the holders of prize fellowships is hardly complete—some went off to climb mountains. The rest of the passage is, however, interesting. "The result of this [English] method of higher education was even more aristocratic than the German or French system. We did found a few fellowships as prizes for men who should manifest in their graduate work the highest powers of research, and we decided to require of such fellows some instruction to the regular students of our school, so as to give them some training as teachers. We limited the instruction, however, in amount, so as not to take the time of the fellow from his research work, and we required that the instruction in every case should be the product of his own research. We thought in this way to combine the excellences of the English fellowship system and the German Privatdocent system. Our plan worked very successfully. Through it we trained up new officers for our own school and for many other institutions throughout the country."

31. Of course, one could argue that universities were created and colleges transformed by the same tendencies—such as the development of science. For my purposes it makes little difference.

3. Remote utility is quite as worthy to be thought of as immediate advantage. Those ventures are not always the most sagacious that expect a return on the morrow. . . . So is it always in the promotion of science.

4. As it is impossible for any university to encourage with equal freedom all branches of learning, a selection must be made by enlightened governors, and that selection must depend on the requirements and deficiencies of a given people in a given period. There is no absolute standard of preference. What is more important at one time and one place may be less needed elsewhere and otherwise.[32]

And he applied these observations to the creation of Johns Hopkins with a grand simplicity:

The Johns Hopkins University: what will be its scope? The trustees have decided to begin with those things which are fundamental, and move gradually forward to those which are accessory.

They will institute at first those chairs of language, mathematics, ethics, history and science which are commonly grouped under the name of the department of philosophy.

The medical faculty will not long be delayed; that of jurisprudence will come in time; that of theology is not now proposed.[33]

But this use of the traditional organizational distinction in the faculties of German universities did not prevent him, in the argument for priorities which followed, from projecting a road which led through the biological sciences (as peculiarly appropriate preparation for the founding of a medical school) through law and jurisprudence to a grouping of studies concerned with "the history of civilization and the requirements of a modern state," to certain departments of engineering, and even to architecture.[34]

The scope of the university, in short, was the scope of knowledge, and that was coextensive with what could be "investigated." The university was a place in which anything could be studied—both in the sense that it could be investigated scientifically and in the sense that the results of those investigations could be acquired.[35] It is not surprising, therefore, that it also became a place in which anything

32. Gilman, *University Problems in the United States,* p. 18.
33. Ibid., p. 20.
34. Ibid., pp. 21 *et seq.*
35. In 1884 John Burgess published an extraordinary pamphlet entitled *The American University: When Shall It Be? Where Shall It Be? What Shall It Be?* (Boston: Ginn, Heath, & Co., 1884). His formulation of the problem of curriculum depends upon the assumption that investigation was primary. "First, then, the entire realm of the unknown belongs to the university. The

could be studied in another sense: the elective system was a natural consequence of the division of knowledge into specialized investigations. In fact, Eliot—the most prominent apologist of that system in its purest form—reversed the argument, asserting that the elective system made scholarship possible and in effect had made universities, in the proper sense, possible.

The largest effect of the elective system is that it makes scholarship possible, not only among undergraduates, but among graduate students and college teachers. While college curricula were prescribed, and therefore dealt almost entirely with the elements of the subjects taught, there was little in the work of the college teacher which stimulated him to broad and deep intellectual attainments. His college work became an absolute routine. . . . He but seldom became an advanced student or investigator; and when in rare cases he did become a real scholar, it was by force of innate genius impelling him to advanced work under most unfavorable conditions.

Since the elective system has become the general practice of the American colleges and universities, so far as their resources have permitted, the whole aspect of the profession of teaching in the higher institutions of learning has changed. Even the young teachers have received each a competent training in some specialty, while the assistant professor and professors are always chosen from men who have demonstrated their capacity for persistent, productive, scholarly work. A successful professor is an enthusiastic student, an inspiring teacher, and an indefatigable investigator. . . .

It is difficult for the present [1908] generation to imagine the condition of the American colleges when there was no instruction given in any of them beyond the elementary courses in the few arts and sciences which led to the A.B. With few and narrow exceptions, no instruction in arts and sciences that could possibly be called advanced, was given in the American colleges before the Civil War. Down to 1872 there was no systematic provision made at Harvard University for instruction in arts and sciences beyond the Senior year of the College. If any young man wanted

---

prime function of the university is the discovery of *new* truth, and the *increase* of knowledge in every direction. The fitting out of academies and even colleges with extensive laboratories, cabinets, museums, and libraries is a great waste of substance. These things all belong to the university, to be used, not as curiosities to entertain, but as means to new discoveries." This essay is reprinted as Appendix I in Burgess, *Reminiscences of an American Scholar.* The quotation above is found on p. 364.

to pursue the study of literature, history, philosophy, or science beyond the limit set by the requirements for the degree of Bachelor of Arts, he had to go to Europe. No other gain from the elective system can be compared with this development of scholarship in the United States.[36]

Speaking from the vantage point of Harvard, Eliot saw the elective system as a function of affluence and a celebration of freedom.

Looking back on the development of the elective system in the American colleges and universities during the past thirty years, one sees that the rate of the development and the width of the resulting system in each case have been in the main a question of the pecuniary resources of the institution. There is no doubt that a prescribed system is indefinitely cheaper than an elective system; for with only one curriculum of elementary courses to provide, a college can get along with a comparatively small number of inferior teachers. A broad elective system requires many teachers of high quality; a prescribed curriculum needs only a few teachers, and these need not be advanced students or investigators. A professor who gives half his time to advanced work with classes of five to fifteen students is a far more costly article than a professor who deals only with classes of fifty to two hundred students. . . .

Finally, the permanence of the elective system is assured by the demonstrated fact that it provides on a large scale an invaluable addition to human freedom, and provides this precious freedom for the most highly trained, and therefore the most productive and influential persons. When the student of history reviews the great achievements of the human race, he comes to the conclusion that those achievements which have brought deliverance from some sort of terror and oppression, or have been gains for some sort of freedom, have proved to be institutionally the most suitable achievements—one might almost say the only durable.[37]

Others, less favorable to election as a system and perhaps less eminently situated with respect to affluence, saw the consequences somewhat differently. In 1900 Harper addressed the National Education Association on "The Situation of the Small College."[38] In a

36. Eliot, "The Elective System," in William Allan Neilson, ed., *Charles W. Eliot: The Man and his Beliefs* (New York: Harper & Brothers, 1926), 1: 144–45.

37. Ibid., pp. 158–59.

38. Reprinted in Harper, *The Trend in Higher Education*. The quotations which follow are from pp. 349, 364–66, 374–75, 384–85.

characteristically probing argument he analyzed the prospects, noting first the qualifications provided by his experience as student and teacher.

> My student life was divided, my undergraduate work being done in a small college [Muskingum College, New Concord, Ohio], my graduate work in a large college or university [Yale]. My life as a teacher has been almost evenly divided, twelve years having been spent in institutions termed "small" [Masonic College, Macon, Ohio; Denison University, Ohio; Baptist Theological Union Seminary, Morgan Park, Illinois], thirteen in institutions which may be called "larger" [Yale, Chicago].

On the darker side of the picture of small colleges, he noted, among other things, their exclusion from "the tendency toward specialism."

> Already the tendency to specialize is seen at the beginning of the third year of college work. This is the natural result of the privilege of election, and also a necessary result flowing from the large number of subjects offered in the curriculum. The small college does not furnish the opportunity to follow out this tendency. . . . The whole tendency toward specialism, therefore, even when held within reasonable and legitimate bounds, is a movement with which the small college finds difficulty in keeping pace. . . . Instruction higher than that of an exceedingly elementary character may not be provided in a great majority of subjects to advantage, if a college has a smaller attendance than 150 students; and yet of the 480 colleges and universities in the United States, about 160, or one-third, belong to this class.

But the greatest threat was provided by the need for resources adequate to the changing methods of higher education, methods essentially those of the "university idea" and "university work."

> But, after all, the greatest difficulty of the small college is its lack of means with which to do the work demanded in these days of modern methods, the methods of the library and the laboratory. . . . The cost per capita of instruction furnished the high-school students in some of our cities, even where the classes are crowded, exceeds the average cost per capita of the instruction furnished in many of our colleges. The demands of the modern methods have quadrupled the difficulty in this respect. So long as the curriculum could be restricted in large measure to the study of Latin, Greek, and mathematics, no great cost was incurred for equipment; but with the introduction of work in history, political economy, and political science the requirements

for books and periodicals is very great. With the introduction of laboratory work in the various sciences the expenditures for laboratories and equipment are very great. Without money these demands cannot be met, and yet without meeting the demands of the present age our colleges all over the land are graduating students who are impressed with the belief that they have been educated in accordance with modern ideas. An institution consists of the men who make up the faculty, of the buildings, and of the equipment. These, however, can be obtained and maintained only with resources of a liberal character.

The solutions he proposed were bold. Some colleges, if provided with adequate facilities, might survive; some should become preparatory schools; some should become what he called, "for lack of a better term," "junior colleges"; some should, as we would be likely to say, "specialize," though his term was different.

So far as the general plan is concerned, each college is a duplicate of its nearest neighbours. A terrible monotony presents itself to the eye of one who makes any attempt to study the aims and motives of these institutions. All alike try to cover too much ground, and, worse than this, all alike practically cover the same ground. A change in this respect is desirable, and inevitable. This change will come partly in the way of the establishment of colleges for particular purposes; a college, for example, established principally for the study of science; another college established principally for the study of literature; another for the study principally of historical subjects. The principle of individualism, which has already been applied in education to the work of the student and to the work of the instructor, must find application to the work of the institution. . . . The time will come when institutions will cultivate individualism. . . . This will be in striking contrast with the present policy, in accordance with which the most poorly equipped college announces courses in every department of human learning; and students are compelled, in self-defense, to dabble in everything rather than to do work in a few things.

The consequences of all these developments in higher education, for secondary schools—high schools and preparatory schools—were necessarily complex and confusing. Of course there were other interests and purposes transforming those institutions, producing changes which the universities and the changing colleges both resisted and accommodated themselves to in bewildering patterns. In 1908 Flexner produced a polemical little book called *The American*

College: Criticism,[39] and the difficulties of adaptation from both
sides may be seen in its treatment of the relation between the college
and the secondary school. Again there enter the characteristic notes
of "individualism" and "election" (of which in an important sense
he is very critical):

> Now, in order to enable the secondary school to locate the
> individual and to carry forward his development on appropriate
> lines, the radical colleges have made away with the traditional
> curriculum imposed indiscriminately on all alike. They have sub-
> stituted for it a considerable range of choices from among which
> a curriculum adapted to their purpose can, it is supposed, be
> framed. Does this scheme, plainly devised as a basis for the
> elective system, accomplish what it intends? I shall try to show
> that its flexibility is apparent rather than real; it is therefore at
> this point the less necessary to point out that even flexibility
> will not alone solve the problem that the college elective system
> imposes on the secondary school.[40]

For this purpose he examines the Harvard entrance requirements—
arguing that "what is true of them applies with equal force" to
Cornell, Columbia, Michigan, "and others."

> Thirty-odd subjects covering an exceedingly wide field enter
> into the Harvard entrance scheme; many of them are there for
> the first time accorded academic recognition. Side by side with
> time-honored veterans like the classics and mathematics, new-
> comers like music and blacksmithing are made at home. To
> each subject is assigned a specific value, estimated in points,
> according to its difficulty or importance . . . Here, then, one
> might say, is abundant elasticity; even should the boy enter the
> preparatory school unexplored or untrained, aimlessness must
> there cease: for Harvard imposes a definite task on secondary
> education and provides an organizable curriculum whereby to
> attain it.
>   Alas, it does no such thing! Closer inspection discloses the
> fact that what one hand offers, the other withdraws. The elective
> range, within which the school is supposed to accomplish the
> student's continuous and purposeful development, is largely
> nominal. Of the 26 points needed for entrance, at least 18 are
> absorbed by studies required by everybody alike . . . Prescribed
> are English, Latin or Greek, French or German, Ancient or

39. New York: Century Co., 1908.
40. Ibid., pp. 73–74.

Modern History, Algebra, Geometry and one Science. Now, consider this conglomeration from the standpoint of college need; is it possible to see in it any pervading purpose? To what has it reference? Certainly not to the ascertaining or definition of individual power, which the college presupposes. Nor does it, as a collection, embody the elements underlying the general social life, and therefore, claiming the warrant of social necessity. The fact is, no rational basis whatsoever can be made out for it, either from the individualistic or social standpoint. It is, in the main, simply the old fixed curriculum that is deemed to have been displaced; an arbitrary, though easily explicable, combination of unrelated and jarring items: English, for example, enters for practical reasons; Latin or Greek is a concession to the educational Tories; and mathematics offers homage to "drill." Every item is a separate scrap; the whole is a patchwork, suggesting in its method of composition, a political platform rather than a rational educational program.[41]

It is not surprising that these shrewd remarks are to a considerable degree still applicable. In the large the problem was clear enough. Election was simply the response to the problem presented by the necessity to *select* among the numerous and continuously increasing alternative lines now available for study and investigation in the world of knowledge and research. Given a sense of direction, much would fall into place. Eliot defended the elective system partly on the ground that once a direction was chosen much became required. But in Flexner's view—and those of others—in its pure form it threw the whole burden upon the student. One could defend this as a kind of experience designed to develop a responsible and prudent exercise of individual freedom, but there were, of course, other considerations, such as efficiency and the discouragement of idleness and dilettantism. In any case the absence of any definable objective left the secondary school in its "preparatory" role rudderless. College curricula might seem equally purposeless and therefore indefinable in the absence of a goal beyond themselves, and that goal seemed to be offered only by a "speciality" or a "profession." Having in effect redefined and expanded the intellectual world in its institutional embodiment, the founders of "the university" had, it would appear, deprived it of any purposeful structure.

41. Ibid., pp. 74–77.

2

The Founders: Democracy

The advancement of knowledge, or of learning, investigation, and research, is of course, itself a purpose, and it is not unusual that in the pursuit of one purpose the conditions of achieving others are altered. The idea of the university and university work was itself an assumption of purpose and function; was it, *is* it, not sufficient? The founders were not sure. They were acutely conscious of the relation of knowledge and intelligence to purposes and activities other than themselves, and it was clear to them that the university, and by consequence the whole of that intellectual activity which they were so busily reconstructing, served purposes larger than it could itself encompass. But the relative clarity of their convictions about the idea of university work was not matched by a comparable directness of expression on the relation of this work to other functions and activities. Some things seemed clear; others were more difficult to identify; the future was difficult to project. They confessed to the uncertainty, but—perhaps unlike ourselves—they seemed confident of the result.

Something of the certainties and the uncertainties, and of the fundamental confidence as well, is to be found in Harper's brief address at the twenty-fifth anniversary celebration of Johns Hopkins, from which this inquiry began. The "University idea [had], beyond question, established itself upon a strong foundation. . . . the spirit of research, once hardly recognized in our higher educational work, is now the controlling spirit, and opportunities for its cultivation abound on every side." A new, a "second period," was beginning. What would it bring? Assuming the prophetic role, he saw "greater development": "Up to this time we have known what could be done by a university with an annual expenditure of one million dollars or so. In this next period, there will be institutions which will have ten millions of dollars with which to conduct a year's work. This will mean not merely growth, but in large measure, reorganization." It would see, then, "greater differentiation": clearer separation of college and university work, of high school and college, and division of labor among institutions at the same level. Further, "the United States will receive proper recognition for university work": he could foresee a time ("near at hand") in which "the students of European countries will take up residence in our American Universities." But more relevant to our present purpose is the vaguest and yet perhaps the most pregnant of his prophecies.

The new period will see an intermingling of University work and University ideals in all the various activities of our national life; in the business world, in the political world, and in the literary world. The old idea of separation from the world at large is fast disappearing, and the new day has already dawned, in which the University is to do notable work in fields hitherto almost unknown; and by methods hitherto almost untried.[1]

Every age has its sense of tis own sophistication in comparison with others—and also its own unrecognized simplicities. It may strike *us* as somewhat naive that after Harper's address, it is recorded, "the audience rising, joined the University Glee Club in singing 'My Country, 'tis of Thee,' after which the meeting was adjourned to the following day."[2] Yet Harper had pointed to an American achievement which in his view altered the status of the United States among the nations of the world—especially in relation to the parent European stem—and he had discerned a potential for notable contributions "in all the various activities of our national life" consequent upon the establishment of the university as an American institution. The Europeans would come to sit at our feet,

1. I quote from *Johns Hopkins University: Celebration of the Twenty-Fifth Anniversary of the Founding of the University and Inauguration of Ira Remsen as President of the University* (Baltimore, 1902), pp. 58–62. (The address is reprinted in Harper, *The Trend in Higher Education*, in a slightly altered form.)

2. Ibid., p. 63.

as we had for so long sat at theirs,[3] but universities were not merely
to be status symbols or cultural ornaments; they were to be instrumentalities for the transformation and enrichment of the national
life.

What did he mean by this prophetic aspiration? Some clue may
be provided by the ways in which, in their own time and on their
own terms, the founders set out to establish relationships between
the universities and the "various activities" of their communities.
Sometimes these relationships were conceived very directly. In his
valedictory address as president of Johns Hopkins (on the same
day Harper summed up the past and the future), Daniel Gilman,
asking for the "indulgence of our friends from a distance," recalled
the "efforts which have been made to identify the Johns Hopkins
University with the welfare of the city of Baltimore and the State of
Maryland," noting that the Johns Hopkins Hospital and

> such medical advisers as I have referred to are not the only
> benefits of our foundation. . . . The promotion of sanitary reform
> is noteworthy, the study of taxation and in general of municipal
> conditions, the purification of the local supply of water, the
> advancement of public education by courses of public instruc-
> tion offered to teachers, diligent attention to the duties of charity
> and philanthropy, these are among the services which the faculty
> have rendered to the city of their homes. Their efforts are not
> restricted to the city. A prolonged scientific study of the oyster,
> its life history, and the influences which help or hinder its produc-
> tion, is a valuable contribution. The establishment of a metero-
> logical service throughout the state in connection with the
> Weather Bureau of the United States is also important. Not less
> so is the Geological Survey, to promote a knowledge of the
> physical resources of the State, exact maps, the improvement of
> highways, of conditions favorable to agriculture, and of deposits

3. In his inaugural address as the second president of Johns Hopkins on
the day following Harper's speech, Ira Remsen produced statistics provided
by the United States Commissioner of Education which in effect showed
how the American universities were faring in relation to the German universities. He gave the number of graduate students in the United States in
1850 as 8, in 1875 as 399, in 1900 as 5,668. Figures for American students in
German universities were, in 1835, 4; in 1860, 77; in 1880, 173; in 1891, 466;
in 1892, 383; in 1895, 422; in 1898, 397. "These figures show clearly that the
increase in the attendance at American universities is not accounted for by
a falling off in attendance at German universities. On the other hand, they
do show that for the last ten years there has been no increase at German
universities, but rather a slight decrease" (Ibid., pp. 78–79).

of mineral wealth, within this region. To the efficiency of these agencies it is no doubt due that the State of Maryland has twice contributed to the general fund of the university.

Nor have our studies been merely local. The biological laboratory, the first establishment of its kind in this country, has carried forward for many years the study of marine life at various points on the Atlantic and his published many important memoirs, while it has trained many able investigators now at work in every part of the land. . . . Here was the cradle of saccharine, that wisely diffused and invaluable concentration of sweetness, whose manufacturers unfortunately do not acknowledge the source to which it is due.[4]

One can see here the inevitable mix of tendencies which later so clearly emerged, especially in the state universities, as a dedication of the university's energies to serving the needs of the community which directly supported it. The ambiguities of this relationship have been much explored in the succeeding years, not only in relation to private donors and state governments, but latterly in relation to the federal bureaucracy and Congress. What should be kept in mind, perhaps, is that from the beginning the universities invited these relationships and in effect offered their services to the community.[5] Nor was this effort some sort of accomodation to

4. Ibid., pp. 30–31. Gilman's reference to saccharine is apposite not only because it involved his successor, Remsen, but because the story (the legend?) involved is one the elements of which have endlessly repeated themselves in the intervening years. Hugh Hawkins recounts it briefly in his account of the early years of Johns Hopkins: "Among the various investigations that Remsen had mapped out was one involving the oxidation of derivatives of toluene. . . . Part of this research, in 1879, was being carried out by a fellow in chemistry, Constantine Fahlberg, a German with a Leipzig Ph.D. Some of the resulting compound stuck onto Fahlberg's fingers. He stuck them into his mouth and tasted an intense sweetness. The tale as told in the chemistry department is that Fahlberg caught the first train to Washington to patent the substance. Although the discovery was published in February, 1880, with Remsen and Fahlberg as joint authors, it was Fahlberg who made the fortune with the industrial development of the new sweetening. . . . In spite of the ill will that developed between Remsen and his student as to who deserved the credit, the university stressed the event as a utilitarian justification for its nonutilitarian methods." (Hawkins, *Pioneer: A History of the Johns Hopkins University, 1874–1889,* [Ithaca, N.Y.: Cornell University Press, 1960], p. 141.) It appears that Fahlberg was actually a Russian trained in Germany.

5. In what follows I have largely used Gilman and Harper, but it should not be concluded that it was only the representative of the "new" universi-

the necessities of survival and support: it was, at least in part, the
expression of a deeply felt obligation inherent in the nature of the
intellectual enterprise. The motto of the University of Chicago,
Crescat scientia, vita excolatur ("Let knowledge grow from more
to more, and so be human life enriched"), for all its ambiguity, is
neatly, and also ambiguously, complemented by the motto of Johns
Hopkins, *Veritas vos liberabit*—a shortened version of John 8:32,
"And ye shall know the truth, and the truth shall make you free."[6]

We have noted above the easy transition Gilman was able to
make, in his inaugural address twenty-five years earlier, from "all
sciences are worthy of promotion" through "remote utility is as
worthy to be thought of as immediate advantage" to "as it is im-

ties who shared these sentiments. (In an important sense, of course, all the
universities were new.) Eliot on occasion could discern the same changes
and fervently join in the aspirations they served. Speaking at the dedication
of Columbia's new (Morningside) campus in 1896, he congratulated New
York because "Its chief university is to have here a setting commensurate
with the worth of its intellectual and political influence. No American community can profit so much from the presence of a strong and progressive
university as can this great city, at once magnificent and squalid, majestic and
ignoble, at once Freedom's pride and Freedom's reproach. Universities are
no longer merely students of the past, meditative observers of the present,
or critics at safe distance of the actual struggles and strifes of the working
world. They are active participants in all of the fundamental, progressive
work of modern society. By spoken word, by pen and pencil, through laboratories, libraries, and collections, through courts, churches, schools, charities,
and hospitals, they promote the forward movement of society and help to
open its onward way. Columbia University, in its recent history, amply
illustrates this truth; for it has contributed effectively to the advancement of
architecture, pedagogy, economics, political science, sociology, chemistry,
physics, engineering, and biology, in all which subjects the city of New York,
and the country at large, have interests of incalculable magnitude." (Charles
W. Eliot, "An Urban University," in *Educational Reform;* pp. 396–97.) He
went on to argue that "the influence of Columbia, and of all well-conducted
American universities" would increase, since "our free institutions are going
to receive a great service from the universities they have fostered." Questions
concerning "independence, union, personal liberty and religious toleration"
depend for their decision on "just sentiments, widely diffused through the
mass of the people," but when public policy depended upon "careful collection of facts, keen discrimination, sound reasoning, and sure foresight," the
republic was necessarily dependent upon experts. "Questions of currency,
taxation, education, and public health . . . require for their satisfactory
settlement the knowledge and the trained judgment of experts; and the only
wise decision which universal suffrage can make upon them is the decision
to abide by expert opinion . . . Now, the experts needed are going to be
trained in the American universities" (ibid., p. 398).

6. The Vulgate has *"Et cognoscetis veritatem, et veritas liberabit vos."*

possible for any university to encourage with equal freedom all branches of learning, a selection must be made . . . and *that selection must depend upon the requirements and deficiencies of a given people at a given period*. . . . What is more important at one time and place may be less needed elsewhere and otherwise." It is not inconsistent, therefore, that in his valedictory he could move easily from the attention given to the oysters of Chesapeake Bay and that "wisely diffused and invaluable concentration of sweetness," saccharine, to less local and less immediately useful considerations.

In the physical laboratory, light has been thrown upon three fundamental subjects:—the mechanical equivalent of heat, the exact value of the standard ohm, and the elucidation of the solar spectrum. For many years this place was the chief seat in this country for pure and advanced mathematics. The study of languages and literature, oriental, classical and modern, has been assiduously promoted. Where has the Bible received more attention than is given to it in our Semitic department? where the study of ancient civilization in Mesopotamia, Egypt, and Palestine? where did the Romance languages, in their philological aspect first receive attention? To American and institutional history, persistent study has been given. Of noteworthy significance also are the theses required of those who are admitted to the degree of Doctor of Philosophy, which must be printed before the candidate is entitled to all the honors of the degree.[7]

The transition made in the last sentence above is not an awkward one, given the assumptions on which Gilman's conception of scholarship rested. All the founders laid great stress on publication —not merely or even primarily as a way of submitting scholarly work to the judgment of peers, but as a way of making available to the world at large the results of investigation. This function was part of what they thought of as the "diffusion of knowledge," and it was not limited to scholarly publication or even to publication in a narrow sense. Speaking at the Columbian Exposition in Chicago in 1893 as president of the International Congress on Higher Education, Gilman formulated the ideal clearly. The functions of a university were the education of youth, the conservation of knowledge, the extension of the bounds of knowledge, *and* the dissemination of knowledge.

7. *Johns Hopkins University: Celebration of the Twenty-Fifth Anniversary of the Founding of the University and Inauguration of Ira Remsen as President of the University* (Baltimore, 1902), pp. 31–32 (emphasis added).

The results of scholarly thought and acquisition are not to be treasured as secrets of a craft; they are not esoteric mysteries known only to the initiated; they are not to be recorded in cryptograms or perpetuated in private note-books. They are to be given to the world, by being imparted to colleagues and pupils, by being communicated in lectures, and especially by being put in print, and then subjected to the criticism, hospitable or inhospitable, of the entire world. . . . Publication should not merely be in the form of learned works. The teachers of universities, at least in this country, by text-books, by lyceum lectures, by contributions to the magazines, by letters to the daily press, should diffuse the knowledge they possess. Thus are they sowers of seed which will bear fruit in future generations. . . . The widespread demand for university extension shows how intelligent persons who for one reason or another have never received the advantage of university residence are eager to get at the latest, the wisest, the most accurate instructions that can be brought within their reach. But learned publications, containing memoirs that are only meant for the scholar,—positive contributions to knowledge,—are the noblest fruits of academic culture.[8]

Harper's plan for the university which was coming to life on Chicago's Midway as Gilman spoke provided a comprehensive recognition of this function. The "work of the university," as he projected it, was to be "arranged under three general divisions, viz., The University Proper, The University Extension Work, The University Publication Work." The university proper consisted of the academies, the colleges, the affiliated colleges, and the schools. The purpose of the university extension work was vigorously—one might almost say evangelically—set forth by Harper in the series of bulletins he published before the university opened.

To provide instruction for those who for social or economic reasons cannot attend in its classrooms is a legitimate and necessary part of the work of every university. To make no effort in this direction is to neglect a promising opportunity for building up the university itself, and at the same time to fall short of performing a duty which from the very necessities of the case is incumbent upon the university. It is conceded by all that certain intellectual work among the people at large is desirable; those who believe in the wide diffusion of knowledge regard it as necessary; all are pleased to see that it is demanded. This work while it must be in a good sense popular, must also be systematic in

8. Gilman, *University Problems in the United States,* pp. 297–98.

form and scientific in spirit; and to be such it must be done under the direction of a university, by men who have had scientific training. For the sake of the work it should in every instance come directly from the university, that thus

1. There may be proper guarantee of its quality.
2. Character may be given it.
3. Continuity may be assured.
4. Suitable credit may be accorded.

The doing of the work by the university will

1. Do much to break down the prejudice which so widely prevails against an educated aristocracy.
2. Give to a great constituency what is their right and due.
3. Establish influence from which much may be expected directly for the university.
4. Bring inspiration to both pupil and professor in college and university.
5. Bring the university into direct contact with human life and activity.[9]

The conjunction here of the ideas of "sciences" (in the broad sense we have noted above) and what can properly be called "democracy" is evident also—in a less aggressive fashion—in the description of the university publication work in the first *Annual Register* of the university.

> In the constitution of the University, special emphasis is laid upon research and investigation. It is not enough that instructors in a University should do merely the class and lecture work assigned them. This is important, but the institution will in no sense deserve the name of University, if time and labor are not also expended in the work of producing that which will directly or indirectly influence thought and life outside the University. . . . The University, including every member of the University, owes to the world at large a duty which cannot be discharged in the ordinary class-room exercise. The true University is the centre of thought on every problem connected with human life and work, and the first obligation resting upon the individual members which compose it is that of research and investigation.[10]

9. *Bulletin No. 6*, June 1892, as quoted in *The President's Report, July, 1892–July, 1902*, p. 304.

10. *Annual Register, 1892–3* (Chicago: University of Chicago, 1893), p. 209.

That this responsibility was not taken lightly is apparent from the description which follows of the new *Journal of Political Economy.*

> The momentous character of the financial questions of the day accentuates in a striking way, not only the importance of training for their discussion, but also the importance of a ready means of connecting experts and investigators in these practical economic subjects with the general reading public.
> It is the aim of the new JOURNAL OF POLITICAL ECONOMY to meet this need. It brings to its pages the work of the economists best fitted to treat special topics from all parts of the world; and these are presented in a clear and readable manner, avoiding all unnecessary scientific nomenclature, yet presenting only scientific results. . . . The value of the JOURNAL, therefore, to *bankers, men of affairs, publicists, students, and teachers* goes without saying. In this day of many complex demands on busy men, it is of first importance to have at hand a journal of the highest standards which is devoted to the sifting and publication of facts and arguments, which are vital to the questions every day touching business life in regard to banking, money, railway transportation, shipping, taxation, socialism, wages, agriculture, and the like.[11]

The Biblical World, which Harper himself founded and edited until his death, received an elaborate description in the first *Annual Register;* a few years later the text had been considerably condensed. The simple statement that the purpose of the journal was "to *popularize* the methods and results of the best biblical scholarship" was not found to be embarrassing.[12]

Perhaps the most immediate, the clearest and most successful attempt—though again the result is not without ambiguity—to transform and enrich the "various activities of the national life" was the effort to enlarge the ambience of the university to comprehend the

11. Ibid., p. 210.
12. See, for example, *Annual Register, 1896–97,* p. 124 (my emphasis). The complexity of purpose and the recognition of the problem involved is clear in the description of the *American Journal of Sociology* which appears in the *Register* in these years. "The policy of the *American Journal of Sociology* is: 1) to be in a restricted sense a popular educator. With this end in view the Journal aims to keep its readers informed about the maturest thought of the world on all subjects with reference to which every member of a self-governing political society should be intelligent. 2) to assist in organizing the work of specialists in the various social sciences by exhibiting the interrelations of results in the different departments of abstract and concrete social sciences; to serve as a clearing house for purely technical sociology." (Ibid., p. 123).

professions, not merely the traditional German "learned professions" of law, medicine, and divinity, but the emerging professions of a different society and a differently constituted culture. Typically the founders started from the German base, but they rapidly moved beyond it: "The medical faculty will not long be delayed; that of jurisprudence will come in time; that of theology is not now proposed," said Gilman in his inaugural; but as he projected this growth, he moved beyond it to speak of engineering and architecture, noting that "there are now, in this new country where so much building is in progress, but two schools for the professional study of this the first of arts."[13] Harper's plan, as we saw earlier, was from the beginning more precise: the university was to include schools of divinity, law, medicine, engineering, pedagogy, fine art, and music. In fact, neither university has realized its original plan; and both have in time acquired professional schools not contemplated by their founders.[14]

The assumptions on which the incorporation of professional schools into the university was grounded were passionately set forth with respect to the traditional faculties of the German universities by John Burgess in 1884.

> The Philosophical faculty is the life and glory of the university. It is the foundation for everything further. Without it, theology becomes a dreary dogmatism, law a withering letter, and medicine a dangerous empiricism. It is possible to have a theological school which is no *university faculty* of Theology at all. In fact, most of the theology schools in the United States are not; and for the simple reason that there is no Philosophical faculty connected with them to furnish the broad basis of psychology, logic, history, literature, and philology, upon which all development and progress in theology must rest. The mere acquirement of creed and ritual is not university theology. It is only the technique of theology. Likewise we may have a law school which is not a university faculty of jurisprudence. Few, if any, of our law schools have risen to the dignity of such a place. Cases and rules of practice make up the substances of the instruction which the pupils want and which the professors usually give. But this, again, regards law only as a bread and butter industry. This is again technique, but not jurisprudence. The Philosophical faculty, again, must place the broad basis of history, logic, ethics, and

13. Gilman, *University Problems in the United States*, p. 26.
14. Chicago, for example, now has a School of Social Service Administration and a Graduate Library School, to say nothing of a School of Business. Johns Hopkins possesses a School of International Studies.

philosophy under the rules and judgments of courts before the law school is entitled to be called a faculty of jurisprudence. The same is true in regard to the School of Medicine. It will stagnate and degenerate into a machine for grinding out half-fitted practitioners unless the chemistry, botany, anatomy, physiology, logic, and psychology of the Philosophical curriculum give it the life and energy for an ever continuing development.[15]

The function of a professional school in the proper sense, therefore, was not to pass on techniques or lore, not to train adequate practitioners replicating the existing professionals, but to engage in a continuing redefinition of the scientific base on which techniques and practice rest: they were to be places in which the profession was itself critically examined and intellectually restructured. The agenda thus set for the university professional schools was not simple, and from the beginning the appropriate difficulties emerged. Some sense of the strain is conveyed by Harper's many discussions about the professional school in which he was personally concerned—the divinity school. These prescient papers[16] reveal a man grappling with resistances both within and without the university, difficulties complicated, in the case of divinity, by questions of orthodoxy and sectarianism. It would be pointless to engage in a lengthy exposition of what is still a very lively debate; some of the issues and the way in which Harper saw them relating to the university idea and university work emerge in what are almost random quotations from his *Decennial Report.*

> The interest of the University is distinctly in a School of Theology which shall partake exclusively of a scientific character, while it is also within the scope of the University to develop a School of Theology which shall emphasize the practical side of this work. It is a question whether both of these things can be accomplished in the same school.
> The subject of theology in its broadest scope, and viewed from the scientific point of view, is one which may not be limited by the influence of a single denomination, nor indeed by any

15. John W. Burgess, *The American University,* pp. 15-16. This essay is reprinted as Appendix I in Burgess, *Reminiscences.*
16. See the following speeches and essays reprinted in Harper, *The Trend in Higher Education:* "The University and Religious Education," "Why Are There Fewer Students in the Ministry?" "The Theological Seminary in its Civic Relationship," "Shall the Theological Curriculum be Modified, and How?"

group of denominations. Such work should indeed be established and may be independent of denominational influence. . . .

A rearrangement of the work in the Departments of Homiletics, Practical Theology, and Sociology, as presented to the Divinity Students, seems necessary. This rearrangement, under what might be called the Department of Practical theology, is, however, something quite different from the proposition to draw a line between scientific and practical Divinity. In this case reference is made to the Department concerned; in the other, to the methods of work in all the Departments of the Divinity School.[17]

Anyone familiar with the thought of John Dewey will not be surprised to find him an eager coadjutor in the work of extending the range and influence of "inquiry." In fact, in this context, so preoccupied with the mutual relations of knowing as an activity and the other activities of human life, his pragmatism appears almost as a simple expression of the university *Geist*. The themes which have recurrently emerged in this inquiry are, it is true, given a special interpretation in his work, but at first sight they seem merely to be formulated there with a kind of reflective clarity. The generalization of scientific method to envelop activities and problems far beyond the scope of "nature;" the interpretation of science as an "ongoing inquiry" to be conceived of as a "mode of practice" or, alternatively, as the "funded results" of previous inquiry on which we draw in the construction of hypotheses for the solution of new problems; the insistence that the controlled reconstruction of the human environment, of human action and human community, was identical with the processes of inquiry and knowledge; and the reiterated concern that the identification of theory and practice produce not a mindless, short-run effectiveness in action, but a reconstructed intellectual world in which the function of intelligence was to be fundamental to all human activity—all of these elements may well appear almost as inevitable in the burgeoning institution which was Harper's new university. It is often said that Americans have a naive and touching faith in the effectiveness of education for the solution of all problems, but the faith on which the new universities was grounded was not really a faith in education: it was a faith in the ability of controlled, scientific inquiry to change the conditions of human life and work. The university was to be the agency of that change, not primarily because it was an educational institution, but because it "is the centre of thought on

17. *The President's Report, July, 1892-July, 1902,* pp. lxxiv–lxxv.

every problem connected with human life and work" and because "the first obligation resting upon the individual members which compose it is that of research and investigation." Characteristically, what seemed necessary was a new, scientifically constructed theory of education—a theory grounded in experiment and formulated as a transformed practice. In such an environment it hardly seems possible to determine whether Dewey's educational theories were a consequence of his philosophy, or his philosophy a mere generalization of his educational theories. And the success of his educational ideas in transforming a profession and the structure of institutions is an astonishing example of the capacities of "inquiry," originating in universities, to remake the world.

There was here an educational problem, but the problem of re-educating teachers and reorganizing schools was initially the same as the problem of establishing education as a university discipline, of organizing an inquiry into educational processes and goals within the intellectual ambience and drawing upon the intellectual resources of the university. In September 1896, in the *University of Chicago Record,* Dewey published a kind of prospectus of this effort, "Pedagogy as a University Discipline," which is one of those writings that may justly be called seminal. It is extremely difficult to represent this article by quotation, partly because it is a shining example of that dogged clumsiness of style which is so characteristic of Dewey's work. Yet so great are its interest and importance as a prime example of the focusing of thought in the creation—or re-creation—of a practice and a profession which the notion of university work required, that at some risk of injustice and redundancy I shall attempt quotation, selecting those passages most relevant to this inquiry.[18]

Harper saw a division of labor between schools of "scientific divinity" and "practical divinity"; Dewey sketched a similar distinction. "There must be some schools whose main task is to train the rank and file of teachers." Such schools would impart "discipline along lines already well established rather than to undertake experiment along new lines." But

parallel to such training schools must be those which direct their energies to the education, not of the rank and file, but of

18. John Dewey, "Pedagogy as a University Discipline," *University of Chicago Record,* 1, nos. 25, 26 (1896): 353–55, 361–63. Reprinted (for the first time) in John Dewey, *The Early Works, 1882–1898,* vol. 5 (Carbondale and Edwardsville, Ill.: Southern Illinois University Press, 1972), pp. 281–90.

the leaders of our educational systems. . . . Training schools of this type should and may, moreover, devote themselves more directly to the work of pedagogical discovery and experimentation. . . . [T]his higher type of training must be undertaken for the most part, if it is to be done in America at all, by universities and to a considerable extent as graduate work.

The elitism apparent to us in this division was, in Dewey's mind, required by the nature of American social and political traditions, which are "all against any close, systematic, and centralized direction and supervision of education on the part of a governmental authority. Extreme local self-government has been the rule in education even more, if anything, than in any other part of the American system." If, then, "our educational systems" are in need of "direction and systematization from expert sources," and these are not to be furnished by the government,

[i]t must be assumed with the authority of science, if without that of bureaucratic control. The universities are the natural centers of educational organization, unless the chaos of extreme centrifugal force is to continue indefinitely. It is for them to gather together and focus the best of all that emerges in the great variety of present practice, to test it scientifically, to work it into shape for concrete use, and to issue it to the public educational system with the imprimatur, not of governmental coercion, but of scientific verification.

The university was the "destined place" for this higher training, for reasons related to much broader intellectual developments.

A reorganization of the educational system is already occurring. It is impossible to undertake, here, a complete statement of the conditions meeting fulfilment in this reconstructive movement. One of these, however, is the great intellectual advance of the present century, an advance equally great in the regions of history and of science. The accumulation of knowledge has become so great that the educational system is disintegrating through the wedges of new studies continually introduced. . . . The pressure began in the college and high school. It is now finding its way into the primary grades, partly from social infiltration, partly from the continued pressure from above. . . . [I]f the increased demands, as regards number of languages, range of literary study, of history and of the physical and biological sciences are to be met . . . the response must proceed from changing the methods in the lower grades, and by beginning work along these lines in the primary school—yes, and in the kindergarten. . . . It is a question of the right organization and balance of our entire educational system, from kindergarten to university, both in itself as a system and in its adjustment to the existing social environment.

This reconstruction may go on in a haphazard, an empirical way. . . . Or it may go on with some clear, if flexible, consciousness of the nature of the problem, of the ends to be met, and with some adaptation of means to these ends. The latter conditions ought to be most clearly met at a university, where psychology and sociology are most systematically pursued; where scientific inquiry is at its height and where methods of work are most fully developed.

In the relation of scholars in the universities to the problems of education in the lower grades, Dewey saw the solution to the problems posed by specialization.

[T]he experiment of the introduction of science or history into lower education is a matter of subject matter as well as of method. It is reasonable to suppose that it can most fruitfully and efficiently be attempted where this subject matter is most adequately and accurately represented. One of the difficulties in introducing scientific methods and materials into lower grades is that "facts" are taught which are not facts; or facts are brought in an unrelated, relatively incoherent way; methods are used that are out of date. The child should be started on the most advanced plane, with the least to unlearn and to correct as regards both particular things and methods; with the maximum of attainable accuracy and with a selection of ideas and principles in some ratio to their importance and future fertility. Where specialists abound, where investigations are continually in progress, where the library and the laboratory are thoroughly equipped, is, if anywhere, the place where such requirements are met. On the other side, the necessity of applying a specialized range of considerations to the purposes of education is the best way of preventing the specialist from becoming narrow. Such a task necessitates looking at the special material in the light of both its adaptation to other studies and to human nature. For one danger of higher education, from the point of view of broad human interests, is that with high specialization there is increasing likelihood of the center of scholarship getting removed from the mass of men, and the things of daily life. Culture becomes tangential to life, not convergent. The problem of the application of the results of special research to educational ends compels a generalization both of subject-matter and of interest.

From this unintended anticipation of the problems of general education as they emerged some thirty years later, Dewey turned to the specific questions of the "organization of the discipline of pedagogy."

> There is no German university in which the subject is presented in a way at once detailed and systematic. So far as can be determined in advance of trial, such an organization would include four main lines of discussion and research, all correlated and focussed in a laboratory of a school of practice, experiment and demonstration.
> Of these four lines, two are mainly concerned with administrative, two with the scholastic side of education.

The "administrative side" was to be a double consideration of the history and theory of the school as a "social and political administration." "Historically, we must know how every people that has made a contribution to civilization has administered its educational forces; what practical ideals it has held in view and how it has shaped its means to realize these ideals." Secondly, this institutional study would merge in "the theory of the best attainable organization and administration in our own country under existing conditions."

The "scholastic side" would also be developed in historical and theoretical phases. The "historical development of ideas concerning education" is "an organic part of the record of the intellectual development of humanity," as the history of educational institutions is of its "institutional development." "No reason can be given for neglecting this that would not apply with equal, or greater force, to the history of science or philosophy." The theoretical study required a generalization of this history into an account of the "various systems of pedagogy which have emerged," together with

> a thorough discussion of psychology and sociology in their bearings upon the selection, arrangement and sequence of the studies of the curriculum and the methods required to give them their full efficiency. If we call the corresponding study of the institutional side that of the educational plant, the problem that meets us here is how to utilize this plant, how to get the maximum of value for human life out of it.

Nor would such a study be limited to "methods required in teaching a subject."

> The question of method is impossible of divorce from that of subject matter; it is simply a question of the relation one subject

bears to another and bears to the human mind. It is the subject-matter taken out of the abstractness forced upon it for purposes of its own convenient study and put into its concrete connections with the rest of the world of knowledge and culture and with the life of man in society. There is opportunity and demand here for the most progressive psychology in determining the relation of studies to the mind in its various stages of development. There is need for a comprehensive philosophy in systematizing the relations of sciences to one another, in determining their correlations, and for widest knowledge of the sciences themselves in their details.

But the responsibilities of the university required more of pedagogy as a *university* discipline than historical insight and theoretical systematization.

[E]very university discipline now has its side of research, of investigation, of addition to the resources of the world. Its function is not exhausted in gathering together, systematizing and perpetuating the accomplishments, theoretical and practical, of the past. There remains the responsibility of testing the attainments of the past with reference to the needs of the present; there is imposed the duty of positive contribution of new facts, new principles. The heart of university work resides more and more in the laboratory and in the working equipment of the seminary [i.e., seminar].

Where is this equipment to be found in the case of a department of pedagogy? Clearly in a school which shall test and exhibit in actual working order the results of the theoretical work. . . . The leading ideas must direct and clarify the work; the work must serve to criticise, to modify, to build up the theory.

Such a school would not be merely an instrument of "practice teaching," as in a normal school.

"[P]ractice" in a university school of practice is a word of enlarged sense. It refers not so much to individual pupils [i.e., teacher-trainees] as to the principles which are tested and demonstrated. Such a school is, in the strictest sense, a laboratory. Without it the instruction in pedagogy is in relatively as disorganized a condition as chemistry and physics would be with only lectures and books to depend upon.

That this fact is hardly recognized nominally, and next to not at all practically, simply indicates in how backward a condition the whole scientific organization of education is—how little society is as yet awakened to the possibility of applying scientific methods of inquiry and organization to educational matters. It is not over-sanguine to anticipate a transformation in education similar to that of chemistry when there is consciousness of the possibilities in this direction. . . . There is no doubt that a laboratory of chemistry might be made self-supporting by devoting itself, say to work in dyes or drugs of direct commercial import. Whether the ultimate utilitarian output, to say nothing of chemical truth, would be as great is another matter. It is inconceivable that, in the long run, the needs of the theory of education should be grasped in any less generous and complete a fashion. What is needed is a sufficient beginning to exhibit the importance and the practicality of the work.

The work began. Early in November of 1896 the *University of Chicago Record* contained another contribution by "Head Professor Dewey": "The University School." The laboratory began with thirty-two pupils, "their ages ranging from six to twelve years." Dewey's statement of the purpose of the school was uncompromising.

> The conception underlying the school is that of a laboratory. . . . As it is not the primary function of a laboratory to devise ways and means that can at once be put to use, so it is not the primary purpose of this school to devise methods with reference to their direct application in the graded school system. It is the function of some schools to provide better teachers according to present standards; it is the function of others to create new standards and ideals and thus to lead to a gradual change in conditions.[19]

With the authority of science to "create new standards and ideals," and so new practices, new institutions, new perceptions, new societies—in fact, a new world; it would be difficult to find a more succinct formulation of the changes to be realized by the reception of law, medicine, divinity, education, engineering, architecture, public service, and all the other professions into the university. "All the various activities of our national life" were not only to be enriched; they were to be transformed. Many years later Robert Hutchins was to suggest that Chicago should take as its motto a line from Whit-

19. Dewey, "The University School," *University of Chicago Record,* 1 (no. 32): 417–18. Also reprinted in John Dewey, *The Early Works,* vol. 5, pp. 436–441.

man: "Solitary, singing in the West, I strike up for a new world."[20]
The spirit of Harper and of the younger Dewey lives in that
suggestion.

Dewey was concerned with the consequences of the "knowledge
explosion" of the nineteenth century for the "right organization
and balance" of the American educational system. His attention
was directed at the primary grades, and even the kindergarten, but
it would be erroneous to contend that the problems had been solved
at the collegiate level. We have already seen the elective system
as an accommodation to the enlarging possibilities of study, but
what was elected was, after all, a *course of study* rather than a
random series of unrelated units. Those who were suspicious of
the freedom of the elective system had to provide a purposive structure offering a basis for choice of the components of courses of
study correlative with a sense of direction in the choices. In the
relation of the college to the university and the relation of the university to its responsibilities both in investigation and professional
training in the new sense, it was possible to find a solution—one
which seemed peculiarily fitted to the demands of the democratic
society within which the university idea had now become embedded.
To put it simply, if the function and structure of the university was
defined by its dual responsibility to the demands of investigation
and the "various activities of our national life," the function of the
college would be to prepare students to participate in the activities
of scholarship and in truly professional training, as these were
differentiated within the universities. Collegiate education, in a
word, would all be "preprofessional," provided one recognized that
the function of scholarship and investigation was itself a professional
enterprise and basic to all others. That is not to say that collegiate
education would become pre*vocational;* that would do less than
justice to the transformation of professional and scholarly training which the university idea comprehended. But it would mean
that the colleges would be able to elaborate courses of study which
pointed clearly to functional orientations in the world of knowledge
and, by consequence, in the society within which that knowledge was
to have its transforming and enriching effects. The idea was not so
clear nor so easily implemented as these considerations suggest; but
in the search for a collegiate function in the new world of universi-

20. Whitman, "Starting from Paumanok."

ties, it became, in many different forms, a persistently recognizable tendency.

Of course, discussion of such developments tended to move in institutional terms. The universities were determined to make professional education higher education. To the extent that professional schools became university schools, they tended to become graduate schools and thus to prolong the educational career of students aiming at qualifying for professional work. By insisting upon a college education as a prerequisite of a professional education, the universities had put great pressure upon themselves to shorten the preparatory period. The question of organization and balance thus tended to be discussed as a question of the point at which university work, and preparation for it, could be expected to begin and on what base it could be erected. Necessarily, in such a discussion the relations to each other not only of graduate school and college, but of upper and lower college work and of college and highschool work were central questions. Even such problems as the ages at which American parents and students were willing to send their children away from home (and how far, for how long) could not be ignored.

The history is complex and confusing, but some characteristic responses and results must be outlined, despite the confusing institutional contexts in which they occurred and the academic jargon in which they are stated. Harper, for instance, labored to separate the "junior college" from the "senior college." In his report for 1898–99 he recorded that the university had decided to confer "the title or degree of Associate upon those students who finish the work of the Junior College." His summary of the reasons is instructive. From the "point of view of the student," he argued that

> no important step is taken at the end of the preparatory course. The work of the Freshman and Sophomore years in most colleges differs little in content and method from that of the academy or highschool—except that it is somewhat more advanced; but . . . at the end of the Sophomore year a most important change occurs . . . for it is at this point that the student is given larger liberty of choice and at the same time higher methods of instruction are employed. For the last two years of college work the university spirit and the university method prevail. . . . It is evident that many students continue work in the Junior and Senior years of college life whose best interests would have been served by withdrawal from college. . . . If it were regarded as respectable

to stop at the close of the Sophomore year, many would avail
themselves of the opportunity. . . . Many students who might be
courageous enough to undertake a two years' college course are
not able, for lack of funds or for other reasons, to see their way
clear to enter upon a four years' course. Many, still further, feel
that if a professional course is to be taken, there is not time for
a four years' college course. It is for this reason that, in part, our
professional schools are made up so largely of non-college students. If a student who had in view ultimately the medical, or
legal, or pedagogical profession could make provisions to finish
a course of study at the end of two years, he would be much
more likely to undertake such a course. . . . [M]any students who
are thus led to take a two years' course would be induced . . .
to continue to the end of the fourth year, and in this way many
students of the very highest character . . . would be enabled to
take the entire college course by whom, under present arrangements, such a course would be regarded as impracticable.

From "the point of view of the University," he argued in effect
that this move would encourage that differentiation of *institutional*
function which he thought appropriately correlative with personal
"individualism." "Many academies are able to do, at least in part,
the work of the Freshman and Sophomore years." Until "young
men and women have shown some maturity of character, it is wise
that they should not be sent very far away from home"; academies
and highschools could "perfect their work" so that many young
people "could pursue their education at least to this higher point."
Further,

[a] large number of so-called colleges, which have not sufficient
endowments to enable them properly to do the work of the Junior
and Senior years, should limit their work to that of the Freshman
and Sophomore years. . . . They find it necessary, however, to
give a degree. If they could follow the example of a large institution and give an appropriate recognition of the work of the
lower years, they would be ready to adopt such an arrangement.
. . . Ninety percent of all the students in American colleges are
to be found in colleges which are within a hundred miles of home.
If a fair proportion of these institutions were to limit themselves
to the work of the Freshman and Sophomore years, at the end
of this time the students who . . . desired to continue would be
compelled to go away from home to some distant institution . . .
in which library and laboratory facilities might be found which
would make possible the doing of good work. If, on the one

hand, the academies and highschools were elevated, and if, on
the other hand, the scope of work done by many colleges were
limited, and as a result institutions developed which would do
that work thoroughly, there would come to be a recognized distinction between college and university which does not now
exist.[21]

It is tempting to sum up Harper's proposals as an assimilation
of the first two years of college to the highschool (or "academy")
and of the last two years to the university as a professional school,
but while this is true, it ignores the fact that he was not proposing
an assimilation to these institutions *as they existed*. The "entire
educational system" was changing, and he was proposing a direction for the change in all the elements, looking toward a clarification of function which would result in that differentiation of institutional character which he consistently prophesied and sought. But
it is nonetheless significant that college was assimilated on the one
hand to preparatory work of a vaguely general character and on
the other to curricula consisting of the more elementary aspects of
professional programs.

The terms in which such curricula were described are worthy of
some note. It was assumed—at least by Harper—that they would
perform a dual function: on the one hand they would prepare for

21. *The President's Report, July, 1889–July, 1899* (Chicago: University
of Chicago Press, 1900), pp. xx–xxi. These recommendations were coupled
with suggestions designed to shorten the course of professional education by
having students enter upon it earlier in virtue of a compression of elementary
and secondary school education and by having professionals return to the
university at appropriate intervals to "gain an impetus which will make it
possible for them to prolong their professional life advantageously to an
older age." As always, Harper was radical and sanguine: "It is unquestion-
ably true that in the period of elementary and secondary education two or
three years are lost in the life of every pupil. There is no good reason why
students should not be prepared for entering college at the age of sixteen,
while as a matter of fact the average age in most institutions is nineteen. Here,
first of all, a change must be introduced. The waste is involved in lack of
proper correlation of work and in lack of adaptation of the work of the
individual. If, now, this difficulty can be remedied, and if at the same time
a year can be saved without detriment in the college course, it will prove a
distinct gain for the cause of professional education. Twenty-five men out
of every hundred are as able to do the work of the college in three years as
the other seventy-five are able to do it in four; and if, in the case of those
who are preparing for professional life, the more elementary subjects of the
profession may serve also as a part of the college curriculum, another saving
of time is secured." (Ibid., p. xxii.)

a professional curriculum, and on the other they would consist of elements furnishing "that general culture sought in college life." In one form or another this assumption has continued to operate in curricular construction. What is significant is that the ground of selection of elements which are suitable for "general culture" is always to be found in the scholarly or professional direction; in what sense the culture thus remains "general" is somewhat obscure. In the same report from which we have just been quoting, Harper noted progress in this direction, making use of distinctions both powerful and difficult.

> Important steps have been taken during the year to arrange more advantageously the work of students who are preparing to enter upon the field of medicine and also that of students who have in mind a business career. Special committees have been appointed to study and report upon the particular interests of such students, and recommendations have been made which look to an arrangement of courses especially related to these interests. It is generally conceded that courses of instruction may be arranged which will, at the same time, furnish that general culture sought in college life and secure distinct progress towards the life work which the student may have selected. There is, of course, a line to be drawn between courses of this semi-technical character and courses wholly technical. It would seem, however, that elementary courses looking toward law, medicine, divinity, and likewise those relating to the many fields of business activity, may serve both for special preparation and general culture. It is on this ground that such arrangements have been undertaken.[22]

By the last year in which Harper presided over the University of Chicago, these developments had produced a complex series of alternatives for students in the "senior colleges." Disentangling the educational intent from the regulations set forth in the *Annual Register* for 1904–5 is difficult. There were six "senior colleges" (of arts, of literature, of science, of commerce and administration, of religious and social science, and of education); four bachelor's degrees (A.B., Ph.B., S.B., and Ed.B.), distributed in bewildering patterns across the colleges; and arrangements for various alternatives within each college. But in effect the student was offered three possibilities, determined by different groupings of departments in the graduate school of arts and sciences and curricula designed for

22. Ibid, p. xxii.

"special preparation" in law, medicine, divinity, commerce and administration, and education. The three possibilities in what may be called "departmental options" were, roughly, the humanities, social sciences and mathematics without the classical languages, and the physical and biological sciences. In addition, for students admitted to the Law School, "the studies of the last year before receiving the Bachelor's degree may be made identical with the first year of the professional curriculum of the Law School," and arrangements not dissimilar were in effect with the Divinity School.[23]

Harper's successor, Harry Pratt Judson, reporting as acting president in the following year, remarked that "[t]he old superstition that the four college years should be spent in general culture without reference to the bearing of work on future life is by this time nearly, if not quite, obsolete. It is quite possible to attain general culture and yet so to plan a good part of the work that it will lead directly toward a profession already chosen." And he called attention to the fact that the idea was being taken up elsewhere. "In the year 1904–5 the report of the President of Columbia University in the City of New York records a distinct adoption by that institution of some of the essential points in the Chicago plan."[24] In fact, the flexibilities of these devices were, under the aegis of Nicholas Murray Butler, enthusiastically pursued. In 1902 Butler had said that the standard four years was "too long a time to devote to the College course as now constituted, especially for students who are to remain in university residence as technical or professional students." In the succeeding three years he was able to announce plans of "acceleration" and "professional option" which enabled students to complete the course in three years and, for "technical and professional" students, reduced the college requirement, in most cases, to two years. "The Faculty of Columbia College say explicitly that to prescribe graduation from a four year college course as a *sine qua non* for the professional study of law, medicine, engineering, or teaching is not to do a good thing, but a bad thing," he said, and argued that "any culture that is worthy of the name and any efficiency that is worth having will be increased, not diminished, by bringing to an end the idling and dawdling that now characterize so much of American higher education." Two years

23. *Annual Register, 1904-5* (Chicago: University of Chicago, 1905), esp. pp. 70–72.
24. *The President's Report, July, 1905–July, 1906* (Chicago: University of Chicago Press, 1907), pp. 6–7.

earlier the dean of Columbia College had expressed misgivings:
"[I]t would be a melancholy outcome if in efforts to minimize the
time required for the A.B. degree, Columbia College should be sub-
verted or degraded into a mere vestibule to a professional school."
He stated his own position as a dissent "from the opinion sometimes
expressed that the American college has served its purpose as a
'lucky accident' in a transition period, and may now be dispensed
with and its function divided between the high school and the university."[25] The changes were nevertheless made and apparently
were effective. Between 1902 to 1914 Columbia College doubled
in size, but the number of A.B. degrees (that is, nonprofessional-
option degrees) increased hardly at all.[26]

Flexner's book of 1908, *The American College,* was extremely
critical of the elective system and the lack of purpose and structure
which it represented both for the college and the preparatory school.
It was a powerful plea for a redefinition of the collegiate function
and the practical recognition of the integrity of the college's educational function as between the secondary school and the gradu-
ate/professional school. As such, it anticipates with striking clarity
most of what later took shape in the general education movement
of some ten to twenty years later. But in this context what is interesting is that Flexner did not repudiate the general destination of
education that seemed to be emerging as a result of the changes
which we have been discussing. Rather, he argued, they needed to
be completed, to be carried to their proper educational consequences.

> My argument, therefore, contemplates not the abandonment,
> but the completer working-out of modern educational tenden-
> cies. The new insight is indeed fragmentary and unorganized;
> but it is on the right track. It aims to vitalize education; to bring
> the boy's[27] powers to bear; to connect the individual with life.

25. The quotations are all from *Annual Reports,* 1902–5, but I found them
in Lionel Trilling's chapter "The VanAmringe and Keppel Eras" in *A History
of Columbia College on Morningside* (New York: Columbia University
Press, 1954), pp. 30–33.

26. I found this figure in William Summerscales' *Affirmation and Dissent:
Columbia's Response to the Crisis of World War I* (New York: Teacher's
College Press, 1970), p. 114, n. 32. According to Summerscales, the number
of A.B. degrees increased from 84 to 95 in the period.

27. Throughout this work Flexner consistently assumes that he is talking
about a system for the education of men. Women are mentioned (so far as

Our part is not to antagonize a movement so clearly sound and inevitable, but having grasped its purpose, to assist its complete realization.[28]

What were the "modern educational tendencies" as they appeared to this well-informed and shrewd observer? The answer should not surprise us. The American college, he argued, was a conservative institution, originally established to produce the clergymen required to replace those whom the colonists brought with them. Although its functions (and its curriculum) expanded somewhat with time, its conservative character remained fundamentally unaltered.

The gradual expansion of the curriculum . . . betokened no radical enlargement of horizon. Increasing complexity of life, progressive amelioration of manners, made lawyers and gentlemen almost as necessary as clergymen. The college supplied them. They were cast in pretty much the same old dies; at any rate, imbued with pretty much the same old spirit. . . . In course of time the college became somewhat more human, somewhat more gracious, somewhat broader in scope and interest, but hardly less conservative.[29]

In other words, the college had always been a professional or preprofessional institution, in the sense that it prepared for definite positions in society. Its classical curriculum made some sense in this relationship, providing the "learning" appropriate to a clergyman, a lawyer, or a man of leisure. What had happened was not only a transformation of the kind of learning offered—indeed, of the whole conception of the range and character of knowledge—but a rejection of the limiting of the social positions and functions which knowledge and learning supported and defined. Flexner sup-

---

I detect) only twice—once using the example of the admission of women with inadequate backgrounds to Continental universities as impairing the "homogeneity of the student body, without which no lecturer can keep to a uniform level," and once objecting to the waste of the "slender" resources of women's colleges in the establishment of graduate departments in such institutions. The latter point rests on the assertion that "[w]omen are now admitted on equal terms with men to all graduate departments." Curiously enough, I *suspect* that this statement was more accurate when he wrote than it was in many subsequent years, provided, of course, that "equal terms" does not mean "equal numbers."

28. Flexner, *The American College,* p. 21.
29. Ibid., pp. 24–25.

plied his own version of the intellectual and institutional revolution
we have been attempting to grasp: "In the last half century, however, this [conservative] situation has markedly changed. Two fac-
tors, science and democracy, have completely transformed our at-
mosphere and ideals."[30]

Science and democracy: what was meant by "science" we already
know. "Democracy" meant the peculiar conditions under which the
intellectual development of science was to be socially and individually realized in the American context. The conjunction of these
two influences ("so congenially . . . engaged throughout the western world in the task of reconstruction, that the connection between
them seems too deep for accident") had transformed education
and its institutions, the schools, into "engines for the completer sub-
version of the passing order." The peculiarly American flavor of
this transformation came not only from the peculiarities of the
American educational institutions as they faced the choices it posed
but also from the special circumstances of American society.

> American college history has been made rapidly since 1870. The
> general causes, common . . . to the entire western world, have
> been in this country accelerated by local influences. Here a vast
> population but recently freed from disability of one sort or an-
> other found itself in a highly favorable environment just at the
> moment when science was suggesting to industry quick and effec-
> tive methods of turning the situation to account. In its turn in-
> dustry repaid the laboratory by testing its conclusions and pro-
> pounding new and stimulating problems. But educational interest
> has by no means confined itself to the physical sciences. The
> same eager spirit has penetrated other realms; it is re-writing
> history, re-conceiving social theory, working-out a nearer and
> more cogent standpoint in philosophy. All this many-sided activ-
> ity comes to a focus in the college. The curriculum struggles to
> embrace every topic of serious intellectual or practical concern;
> it calls for all possible varieties of individual capacity and pref-
> erence. The reconstructive function of the college is still further
> emphasized by the development, in close connection with the
> college, of graduate schools, borrowing the technique of research
> perfected in Germany, and largely devoted to the discovery and
> circulation of new truth. The contents of college instruction are
> thus, like the waters of a mountain lake, always in process of
> fresh replacement. The college can never again be restricted to

30. Ibid., p. 25.

conservation of a hard-and-fast type, individual and social. It has become one of the main agents of progress and change.[31]

In these circumstances the old classical curriculum, which at best prepared for legal and ecclesiastical careers and embodied a notion of general culture appropriate to an outmoded leisure class of "gentlemen," was as unacceptable an alternative as the pure elective system, which achieved a variety in which the college in effect abdicated its educational responsibility to the "choices" of students. In these circumstances Flexner set himself to state the problem of constructing a collegiate curriculum which would effectively recognize not only (as the elective system inefficiently did) the vocational but "other aspects of individual activity." But the recognition of the needs of individuals was grounded in the requirements of the kind of society within which individual differences and competences could be sustained and individuals flourish.

> An elective system that gives effect only to dominant personal choice loses sight of other not less essential activities. Such activities are indispensably important to fulness and wholesomeness of life; they protect us against such total immersion in special occupations as would threaten to destroy the very basis of interaction among men. . . . It is no foregone conclusion that mere existence within a community will effectively prepare a man for his proper part in its intellectual interests and social struggles. I hold that if a liberal education is anything more than a personal indulgence or a personal opportunity, the college has a very distinct task in reference to the impersonal aspects of social and civic life.[32]

Flexner's analysis of the problem presented to the college—the recovery of liberal education in new intellectual and social circumstances—is an interesting and subtle one, but at the moment what may interest us more is not the special character of his solution but the sense of the problem which he shared with others. "Science" and "democracy" are terms not inappropriate to point to the peculiar quality which the problem had assumed for those who labored in the American educational vineyard, though neither term would mean for them what it might suggest to us. On the one hand they had carried out a reconstruction of institutionalized cognitive activities, creating a structure oriented toward discovery, growth, in-

31. Ibid., pp. 27–29.
32. Ibid., pp. 130–31.

quiry: "research." On the other they attempted to work out the
consequences which this reconstructed cognitive activity would
have for individual competence and social service in a society open
to change and receptive to the "authority of science." Education
was to be—and became—both the subject and the instrumentality
of change. They were not the first to perceive that knowledge as a
human activity has consequences for other activities and that it is
an associated activity which in the interest of continuity and control of its consequences must be appropriately institutionalized.
What they sought to formulate were the demands of a novel conception of cognitive activity and its organization and a novel relation to a society which itself would derive its character from the
growing impact of knowledge on its characteristic activities. The
problem was not a new one; the conditions in which it required to
be solved and the purposes to be realized in it were, in their view,
new. They embraced the problem as an opportunity with enthusi-
asm and confidence.

When Harper, not yet fifty, died in 1906, Albion Small, chairman of the Department of Sociology and founder of the "Chicago
school" of sociology, brilliantly summed up the significance of his
accomplishment in a contribution to a memorial issue of *The Biblical World*. No doubt his analysis of Harper's sense of mission is a
simplified one and inadequate even to the complexities of this individual career and personality. Certainly it cannot be taken as applying simply to the motives, purposes, and intentions of all those
who contributed to the reconstruction I have tried to sketch out.
Yet its lucidity is not wholly deceptive, partly because Small has the
intellectual audacity required to separate purposes and aspirations
from particular institutional arrangements: he is not discussing what
Harper did save in the sense in which we can describe what we are
doing by reference to the ends we aim at and the problems we
address.

> The basis of Dr. Harper's work as President was a daring
> analysis of the whole social situation in the United States. That
> analysis did not go into all the particulars which would interest
> the sociologists. It went far enough to justify in Dr. Harper's
> mind precise convictions about some of the demands upon edu-
> cation that are implicit in American democracy. . . .
> Dr. Harper's analysis of American conditions determined the
> main plank of his working platform; namely, that more and bet-
> ter education is the primary condition of progressive democracy.

Accordingly the central ambition of his life was to do everything in his power to make the educational element in our institutions adequate to the needs of our situation. . . .

Without tracing the influence of his apprentice years . . . , it is easy to define the cardinal aim which shaped his work at Chicago. His imagination had pictured the most important contribution that could be made to American education—a university which would be distinctive in its combination and emphasis of three things. The first was investigation. Every important subject within the possible realm of knowledge should be regarded as a field for research, so far as it presented scientific problems. Not least among the problems which the University should investigate was itself. It should never so far take itself for granted as to presume that its methods were final. Education, from nursery to laboratory, should be treated as a perpetual experiment, and methods should be changed to meet either new conditions or better insight into the conditions. The second trait of the University should be its active ambition for human service. Knowledge for general use, not for the culture of scholars, was the ideal. Scholarship should be promoted as zealously as though it were an end unto itself, but the final appraisal of scholarship should be, not its prestige with scholars, but its value to human life. The University should be, not a retreat from the world, but a base of operations in the world. The third distinctive trait should be accessibility. The University should have more ways of entrance than older institutions had provided, and it should have more direct channels of communicating the best it could give to the world. Besides attempting to reach these special ends, it should do its share of the conventional work of imparting knowledge by the best methods that had been discovered. . . .

In recent years we have become familiar with reflections upon the merits and demerits of the administrative type that is supposed to have supplanted the scholarly type in university presidents. The delicacy of our refinement and the nicety of our discrimination are reflected in the current phrase "the educational boss." Both explicitly and by implication Dr. Harper has been designated, oftener than any other man, as a fair specimen of the type. So far as the facts in his case affect the general question, the type is radically misunderstood, and the epithets used to depreciate it are ignorantly misapplied. Dr. Harper was essentially the leader in an expanding educational experiment. He was the organizer and foremost observer in a co-operative scientific investigation. His work as commissary general for the enterprise was always rated by himself, and was always in fact, subordinate and incidental to the controlling scholarly purpose to increase

knowledge in order to enrich life. Instead of displaying the spirit
of a despot, he was the most zealous and docile learner in the
whole organization. He was not merely tolerant of other views
than his own, but he never assumed the responsibility of a decision about a question of University interests, from the appointment of a docent to the organization of a professional school,
without attempting to exhaust the evidence from every source
that could shed light upon the problem. When the story of Dr.
Harper's life is told in detail, the facts not merely about his departmental scholarship, but about his whole administrative career, will have to be arranged around this central proposition:
His personality was a constant reflection of the faith, "The truth
shall make you free." From first to last, in spirit and in practice,
his central allegiance was to the service of truth.[33]

I see no point in debating the ultimate value of the revolution
carried out by Harper and his coadjutors throughout the "North
American continent."[34] It is sufficient testimony to the magnitude

33. *The Biblical World* 27, no. 3 (1906): 216–19. The issue consists of
a number of contributions, each dealing with a phase of Harper's life and
work. Small's contribution is entitled "As University President." It will not
have escaped the reader that in his final paragraph Small offers an English
version of the University of Chicago motto officially adopted some six
years later: "to increase knowledge in order to enrich life." The only account
I have been able to find attributes the Latin version to Paul Shorey, operating
partly under the influence of Tennyson's line from *In Memoriam,* "Let knowledge grow from more to more." No mention is made of Small in this account.

34. There was a very deep consciousness of regionalism—almost in a
symbolic form—in the minds of many of those who participated in this
revolution. In a passage which I did not quote above from Small's assessment
of Harper's work, he found the "crucial test" of Harper's "fitness to be put
in charge of a great educational enterprise" in his decision to work in the
Middle West. The whole passage is worth quoting. "Not least significant
among the results of Dr. Harper's preliminary survey of social conditions
was his conclusion about the desirable location of the path-breaking University. For several years a plan to plant a new university in an eastern
city had been under consideration. Men of accredited wisdom and large
influence had shared in shaping the project. There were encouraging grounds
for hope that sufficient money could be obtained. Presently it became necessary for Dr. Harper to express his opinion about the scheme. At this point his
study of American tendencies registered a strategic judgment. It involved a
complicated and costly moral struggle, threatening interruption and perhaps
loss of valued friendships, to have the courage of his convictions. It was
even possible that differences of opinion might altogether divert from education the endowments that were in prospect. In spite of personal preferences,
however, and in defiance of inveterate prejudice that dignified American

of their achievement that, some hundred years later, the institutions they created in an attempt to realize their aspirations and solve the problems they saw, remain fundamental conditions of the arena in which we must address ourselves to intellectual and educational problems. Perforce we carry on in the tradition in which, as Small said, "not least among the problems which the University should investigate [is] itself." In large part what there is to investigate is what the founders created. The basic autonomy of the enterprise is its capacity to understand and reorganize itself. In that sense, at least, we may hope that the truth may liberate.

---

leadership must center in the East, Dr. Harper reached the conclusion that the most promising place for a dynamic movement in education was the Middle West. There are good reasons for the belief that this proved to be the crucial test of Dr. Harper's fitness to be put in charge of a great educational enterprise." (p. 218.) This note of western "patriotism" and the challenge it offered to what we would now call the eastern establishment runs through much of Harper's own writing. See, for example, "Dependence of the West Upon the East," an address delivered at the bicentennial of Yale, 1901. "History has always know a Westland," he asserts, but until now it has been an "ever-changing, ever-shifting Westland." The Nile was the first Westland; now the Westland is "the great middle region drained by the Mississippi." But the Middle West, "together with the country still beyond the mountains called the Far West, represents the last step westward to be taken." Throughout these changes the West "has represented relief from the congestion of territory, release from the bonds of conventionalism, freedom from the rigidity of tradition. It has furnished opportunity for effect on the part of those who had tried and failed, and those to whom the opportunity to try had not before been given. . . . It has served as the home and school of democratic ideas; for in the West men have lived more nearly on terms of equality, and in the West there has been a truer exhibition of the spirit of fraternity." (Harper, *The Trend in Higher Education,* pp. 135 *et seq.*)

3

Liberal Education:
A Search for a Problem

I

What we described in the first part of this inquiry was conceived of by those who undertook it as a reconstruction and a reorientation. While they did not claim absolute novelty, they clearly felt that what they were doing was profoundly innovative. But what was it that was reconstructed and reoriented? Most obviously, of course, it was an *institutional* revolution, and we have traced some of the outlines of institutional changes in physical facilities, professional redefinition, the attachment of new sorts of functionaries to the enterprise, and in the outlines of careers patterned by the new institutions for those whose energies they organized—including, of course, curricula for students. Moreover, it was an integral part of the conception of these institutional changes that new relationships to other institutions and forms of organized social activity—in the political, the literary and artistic world, the world of technological and economic activity, and the more traditionally related institutions of the pedagogical and learned professions—should be developed and sustained, so that, as Albion Small put it, the university would be, "not a retreat from the world, but a base of operations in the world."[1] It would be instructive to trace, in these institutional terms, the complex history of what Harper looked forward to in 1902 as a new period in the development of the university idea. How have

1. See chap. 2, note 33.

the universities effectively responded to his prophetic challenge to achieve "an intermingling of University work and University ideals in all the various activities of our national life," doing "notable work in fields hitherto unknown; and by methods hitherto almost untried"?[2] There are those who would argue that we have by now passed into at least a third period of the age of universities: one characterized by a profound disillusionment with the effectiveness of institutions of higher learning as instruments of transformation and reconstruction of our national life. In its back-handed way, this disillusionment (often discovered and confessed) is a tribute to the effectiveness with which the universities as ideas and institutions have impressed themselves upon the society of which they are parts, accepting responsibilities and arousing expectations—always of course, with an infection of ambiguity.

But such a history—fascinating and instructive is it might be—would, in the terms provided for us by the founders, run serious risks of missing the point. It might well, in effect, reverse the priorities which dominated the thinking of those who participated in the invention of these institutional forms and thus made them, for us, part of the data of the problems for the solution of which they had been created. The *institutional* revolution, for them, was the consequence of an attempt to meet the demands of an *intellectual* reconstruction and reorientation—an effort to "institutionalize," to provide the physical and social conditions under which a form of intellectual and educational activity could be stabilized, sustained, and autonomously developed. Universities, as they organized them and as we know them, did not *define* the "university idea" and "university work": they were efforts—always in some degree incomplete and ineffectual—to realize that idea in the organized activities of human beings in specific circumstances. Nor does this way of putting the matter commit one to some form of Platonism: human capacities and functions, to the extent that they are thought to be understood and generalized as to their conditions, may become in the work of mankind guiding ideas which are ideals in a direct and pragmatic sense, requiring for this purpose no further account of their ground or origin. Whether one thinks of the university idea as a Whiteheadian idea having adventures among men and their institutions or as insight into the nature of a successful and satisfying human activity, an insight serving as a guide to efforts to stabilize

2. See chap. 2, note 1.

and sustain that activity, makes, for the purpose in hand, very little difference. In either case the history of the arrangements in which men have responded to the demands of ideas should be informed throughout with the sense that institutional arrangements are analytically and practically posterior to the ideas and purposes they attempt to encompass, even though only in the life of institutions and individuals do these ideas "exist." What we are trying to do is never exhausted in what we actually do. There is no unique relationship of particular means to ends, and the possibility of failure depends upon the assumption that what we do has some standard in purpose—in that sense, prior to it. As Albion Small saw, the university idea itself required constant self-examination and practical redefinition. "Not least among the problems which the University should investigate was itself. It should never so far take itself for granted as to presume that its methods were final. Education, from nursery to laboratory, should be treated as a perpetual experiment, and methods should be changed *to meet either new conditions or better insight into the conditions.*"[3] Of course, it would be unnecessary to reiterate such statements, with their implied warnings and exhortations, were not the power of institutions and habits in confining our imaginations and, in effect, *becoming* our standards equally obvious.

Nevertheless, it behooves us to inquire, with the benefit of hindsight, into the character of the intellectual changes and the intellectual conditions which the new forms of intellectual activity required for their maintenance and development. Libraries, laboratories, and museums—what Harper called the "outside" of university work—are, in a specific setting of human purposes, capacities, and methodical intellectual activities, fruitful materials, but they are powerless by themselves to provide more than indeterminate possibilities. What a library is as a functional instrumentality depends upon what is brought to it in the attitudes and determinate powers of minds. Libraries and laboratories are powerless by themselves to determine directions of research or its results; they do not account for those shifts of interest which make them obsolete or newly relevant in ways unanticipated by their designers. From this point of view the institutions which embodied the university idea were grounded on the assumption that there is an enterprise which is intellectual, and that it requires institutions which organize, sustain, and enlarge

3. See chap. 2, note 33. Emphasis mine.

the work of those individuals who share its purposes and participate in its activities. Those institutions would be institutions among others, just as the community of the learned, the scholarly, and the scientific is a community among the communities which constitute cultural and national communities and in the widening circles of interaction which point to the human community. One way to put the matter simply would be to say that the design of institutions of learning is determined by the demands of scholars and the necessary conditions of their creative work. In one form or another this view has become almost a dogma in the institutions—the universities—which the founders created. For the purposes of apologetic rhetoric, it conveniently overlooks the sense in which the scholar is ineluctably dependent on the intellectual work of others—whether in library or laboratory—to say nothing of those responsibilities he may have to other communities and their institutions. The definition and discharge of these latter responsibilities (which may, from the other side, be seen as the ground of the claim the scholar makes for the resources which support his "independence") was part of the task laid upon universities by the founders.

This is a deceptively simple idea. At the base of the founders' reconstruction of the intellectual enterprise—one is tempted almost to say "of the knowledge business"—there may have lain some one conception of the nature of knowledge, its organization, and its characteristic methods; but this conception is unarticulated, and a developed formulation of it was apparently not felt to be necessary to the institutional and individual reorientation which was in hand. Characteristically the founders thought in terms of the activities of identifiable individuals and groups and sought to provide the conditions which those activities demanded. Insofar as there were methods involved, they were taken as given in what scholars and scientists were successfully doing, or as identified by the instrumentalities —libraries and laboratories—which they employed. From the point of view of a philosophy of science or an articulated epistemology, these formulations therefore seem to suffer from an incorrigible vagueness. It was not that the founders had no sense of participating in and effectuating an intellectual change which had historical and philosophical roots of which they were aware, but rather as if they took that for granted and said, simply, "Here are investigators doing things which are clearly interesting and powerful, things that have consequences for our understanding of ourselves and the world and for the conditions of our living. Let us devote ourselves not to the investigation of the grounds of their action and success but to facilitating their activity." Whether they were pragmatists in some more basic sense than all institution-builders are pragmatists—men of action serving human action, servants of the servants of human enterprise—is a matter for speculation. Some might find this attitude peculiarly American or characteristic of the late nineteenth century, but in any case it is not surprising that in this context John Dewey's attempt to work out a thoroughgoing pragmatic or instrumentalist conception of knowledge and knowing should seem remarkably at home. To conceive of science and knowledge as "modes of action," both in the sense that investigation must be analyzed in terms of the *activities* of investigating and that one cannot locate any discontinuity between theory and practice, between knowing and doing, seems, as we noted earlier, almost like a description of the institutions within which Dewey was working—and which, of course, he was helping to create and recreate. But it is significant also that pragmatism in the sense of a developed philosophy purporting to give an account of what investigators do has come and gone, while the institutions, with much the same operative character, survive.

In this respect, however, the founders may have been wiser than they knew. Whether by accident or design, they were giving practical recognition to a fact about the intellectual world in the sense in which that world is an actual community of working men and women. For in that world there is a radical diversity of intellectual modes—philosophies, conceptions of knowledge, assumptions as to the relations of bodies of knowledge to each other, standards for the recognition of what constitutes a significant result of research, and the intellectual structure of the activities of knowing and investigation. Much of this diversity, of course, remains unarticulated, but it is implicit in the activities of individuals and tends to emerge, usually unidentified, in controversy and in basic difficulties of communication and interaction. From the point of view of any developed philosophical position, the intellectual world in this functional sense is likely to appear an anarchy constituting a community only in some external, institutional sense wherein differences are papered over by inadequate rhetorics. The diversities of philosophies—of logics, of histories of knowledge and science, of metaphysics—are some rough indication of the actually diverse frameworks of ideas within which historians, scientists, humanists work. And, most maddening of all to the philosophic mind, the members of this community frequently seem not only indifferent but actively hostile to the demand that they reflect upon what they are doing and articulate its generic structure. (Less maddening, but discouraging, is the ineptitude and naiveté they display when they attempt reflection.) When, in the thirties, Robert Hutchins told American academic communities of their need for metaphysics, he was pointing to this curious feature of universities, whatever else he may have been doing. His rhetoric may have been ineffective, but the diagnosis of an intellectual situation it reflected was a shrewd one. It was frequently interpreted as a demand for a dogmatic uniformity imposed by speculative thinkers, but as a request for an articulation of grounds and an examination of the problems presented by the differences which would thus be disclosed, it was a serious attempt to encourage the development of the university into a community of scholars of which the community would be grounded in more profound affinities than are provided by buildings, salaries, academic constituencies, and university constitutions and statutes. However, for the purposes of this inquiry the philosophical pluralism of the actual university community is a fact with significant consequences not to be ignored or even deplored.

The intellectual world, then, as an actual community of working individuals and groups of persons is characterized by a double diversity. There is the familiar diversity which is easily (too easily) thought of as a kind of division of labor in the interest of getting the work done—a diversity of subject matters, areas of investigation, or, in terms of the identity of the participants, specializations and specialists. And there is another diversity—less often recognized or discussed—of working assumptions as to the nature of the enterprise, its standards, and the identification and interrelation of its functional parts in the first sense. To the extent that this latter diversity is discussed as a characteristic of the intellectual world, there exists a natural temptation, frequently succumbed to, to identify, in some form, the two kinds of diversity. Analyses such as that capsulized in the phrase "the two cultures" depend upon the assumption that there exists a fundamentally different attitude toward thought and radically diverse conceptions of knowledge and its consequences for human existence in different bodies of knowledge, areas of investigation, and, therefore, between different groups of specialists or scholars. As a statement of aspiration or a formula of conflict between two possibilities—both to some extent actually exemplified—such an analysis is intelligible (if not defensible), but as a statement about the intellectual characteristics of actual scientists, humanists, and (for example) economists, it is a gross oversimplification, doing less than justice to the intellectual attitudes which unite some physicists with some linguists and some economists with some historians as well as to the divisions which make it almost impossible for some linguists to communicate with others. Since this radical intellectual diversity extends even to the terms in which we attempt to define it, it is difficult to point unambiguously to the differences. However, it may be roughly indicated by suggesting that the "two cultures" might be described as "technological" and "intellectual." To argue that this difference corresponds to the difference between science and other disciplines is implausible. There are musicologists who, in their habits of thought, find more in common with some theoretical biologists and some physicists (and can profit more from discussions with them) than they have with their historically minded colleagues. Or again, there are Cartesians in linguistics, anthropology, and physics, and also Baconians in all of them. In such circumstances colleagueship is not easy to trace.

For the purposes of this inquiry it is sufficient, at least at this point, to take note that the university organizes the intellectual world in a division of intellectual labor and necessarily accommodates a plurality of radically diverse intellectual stances and functionings. But in its founding, as we have seen, it embodied another impetus, vaguely referred to as democracy. "Democracy" meant not only that the university was to be accessible to the qualified (and the discrimination and qualifying of them was to be part of its function) but that its activities and their fruits should expand to enrich the lives of men by transforming the culture of the communities of which the university is a part. In part this was to be a literal expansion: all professions and vocations in the culture were to be brought (in their intellectual, thoughtful form, not in their habitual, routine, and technical state) within the institutional ambience of the university, where they could be subjected to the influence of thought and fructified by its methods and results. Such a programmatic aspiration need not rest upon the assumption that all activities are intellectual—purely activities of thought—but it does assume a culture, a way of life, grounded in understanding and insight into itself and its functions and of the world within which it flourishes or perishes. It assumes, in other words, that the stabilization and enlargement of human goods in a culture and a society has as key condition an intellectual culture. In that form such a program is, of course, not a novel conception. What was new—or seemed new—was that this intellectual culture was not to be the privilege of the few, either in its practice or in the enjoyment of its fruits; in that sense it was a democratic ideal.

Again this is a deceptively simple idea, for in effect it prophetically postulated a massive expansion of the intellectual world beyond the institutional expansion of the university. Most directly, it is clear that members of the newly-to-be-sophisticated professions would not cease to be members of the intellectual community when they passed from the precincts of the university into the various activities of the national life. We have already seen how the founders grappled with the problems of maintaining and developing the circulation of ideas within and beyond academic circles: publication was not only for the benefit of scholars in their libraries and laboratories; it was for the widening circles of those who carried the fruits and disciplines of scholarship into other arenas. Of course, there was no simple agreement as to how this permeation of intellectual influence was to be accomplished. Eliot attempted a distinction between kinds of social questions—policy decisions, as we might now call them—which were the proper province of the society as a whole and those more limited questions, within the framework of basic directions, for the resolution of which other communities would have to turn to the experts in and trained by universities.[4] Dewey foresaw an educational system transformed by educators armed, not with the power of government, but with the "authority of science," a source of change and control he thought peculiarly appropriate to a society in which directions were determined by who participated in and were served by the institutions he was setting out to alter.[5] Surely recognition of that authority—receptivity to it—was not to be, *could* not be confined to scholars in schools of education and their well-trained students. And when Harper suggested that university professors who were incapable university teachers might well consult Dewey's department, he was suggesting that expertise in one direction did not confer authority in all, that every scholar was, outside his field, a layman. The burden laid upon "layman" in this sense is an onerous one, since one of the most obvious facts about experts is that they disagree. Unless choices

4. See chap. 2, note 5.
5. See chap. 2, note 18.

among them were to be made by the prestige of their universities, the number of their degrees, or the academic salary and prizes they could command, receptivity to expertise and the authority of science must be based on some appreciation of the force of arguments and the power of analyses to formulate and illuminate problems. To this extent, at least, those who are to profit from expert insight and advice must be participants in the activities from which that competence issues.

Less obvious, perhaps, but just as important, is the burden placed on scholars and investigators by this conception of an enlarged influence for knowledge in a society in which the organs of power and decision are assumed to be amenable only to intellectual authority. It is usually assumed, in one way or another, that communicability is an indispensable mark, though not a guarantee, of knowledge or thought. But communicability within what community? Or, since the relationship is convertible, what community is to be constituted by communication? Implicit in the conception of the university as center of an intellectual life participated in by communities far wider than the academic community is the assumption that scholarship, learning, and science are communicable beyond the circles of those immediately engaged in university work. Yet, as Harper's suggestion about the deficiencies of scholars as teachers again suggests, the disciplines of such communication are not automatically conferred by scholarly competence. The capacity for such communication is not merely an ornament of the scholarly vocation, it is a condition of the *existence* of communities which can fruitfully participate in—practically appreciate, one might say—the scholar's work. Scholars tend to become conscious of this problem only when they realize that they depend upon these communities for support or for a receptivity to the solution of a problem which is not merely the scholar's problem, such as disease or economic chaos. But unless the obligation to make available shareable goods is grounded simply in some formula of quid pro quo or the passionate (in principle, *whimsical*) concerns of individuals, the constitution of such communities by communication is an obligation *inherent in the enterprise of knowing*. It does not follow that everyone in a society must be reached; there are many communities short of the total community. Nor does it follow that the mode of communication must be the same in all communities. The discovery and the articulation of organs and appropriate modes of communication that do not do violence to intellectual integrity is another burden laid upon the universities by the conditions of their activity. The respectable cannot avoid the task of popularization in a community character-ized by popular control and assumed to be amenable to the author-ity of science. It is rather a problem to be mastered, a function to be performed, a discipline to be acquired, an art to be practiced.

II

But all of these considerations, rich and confusing though they may be, do not yet reach the heart of the problem we are exploring. The nature of the intellectual enterprise, even in the operational, institutional, or social terms assumed in the interest of practicality by the founders of universities, imposes responsibilities, in the simple form of indispensable functions, on the community carrying on the work and contributing its fruits to other communities or society as a whole. A considerable transformation of our under-standing of these necessities takes place when we ask not how these functions are discharged by the intellectual community as such but rather how they shape the lives and functional identities of the in-dividuals who, in virtue of *their* work, are or aspire to be members of this community. Our description of the intellectual world so far has been constructed by discovering a series of diversities within it: the plurality represented by subject matters and investigations (spe-cialities); the plurality of philosophical attitudes and assumptions; the plurality of relations to ideas and thought represented institu-tionally, in the world contemporary to the founding of the univer-sities as we know them, by the difference, within the university, of the philosophical and the professional faculties, and in the larger world by the distinction between the academic world and the world of ideas and thought outside the walls of libraries and laboratories in all the activities of the national life. Yet all of these pluralities issue in, are expressed in, and in a very important sense originate in the workings, the intellectual doings, of *individual members of the community,* a community constituted by their ability to carry on and contribute to an enterprise which their individual activity does not exhaust. To put it simply, it is individuals who have spe-cialties and are specialists; it is individuals who work upon assump-tions, implicit or explicit, as to the nature of knowledge and its standards and achievements; it is individuals who in the character of their activity place it in some one of the many possible relations which intellectual activity may bear to human purposes and the many patterns of action in which purposes are realized. *The personal definition of such individuals is that individual conformation in which a vocation is forged within these dimensions of an intellectual culture.*

It is unfortunate that we do not possess adequate terminologies for discussing these vocational possibilities, since insofar as they are truly vocations and not merely appendages to another life, joys and sorrows, failures and achievements, goods and evils reside in them for those whose functionings they are. We may say of someone that he or she has a certain cast of mind, tends to think in a certain way, or reduces all problems and inquiries to a single form. "Interest" is a term which serves multiple purposes in such attempts at characterization. On the one hand it is used to point to a kind of problem, question, or subject matter—a specialty or a direction of research: "I'm interested in why it is that . . ." or "I'm interested in certain things that happened to the novel in the nineteenth century in France." On the other hand it points to the general orientation of thought in another sense. "He is really interested in changing the world," whereas someone else is interested only in the relations of ideas or the precision of their formulation. But these are but crude beginnings of descriptions of intellectual personalities, or "styles," as they are sometimes called. Efforts at further definition are complicated by the inevitable interrelation of these dimensions of the functions of thought. An interest in a certain problem or subject matter is necessarily related to some conception of what is a determinable problem, of the terms in which significant, answerable questions can be formulated, and of the way a subject matter develops or is investigated. And the structure of knowledge and of investigation is profoundly affected by the assumptions one makes as to the ways in which knowledge is a consequence or may have consequences. It is not only the Marxists who have grasped that "understanding" the world and "changing" it may require transformations of how one conceives the world and formulates questions about it. The whole of Dewey's philosophy might almost be read as a commentary on and development of such an insight and intellectual reorientation.

It is obvious that these identifiable, sometimes almost palpable, differences in the conformation of individual minds are at least in part the product of their training, their particular situation in a changing intellectual culture, or, simply, their educations. To say this is not to deny that such differences may also have genetic or natural grounds or that an intellectual culture may be conditioned or determined by other, nonintellectual, circumstances. (Attempts to identify those circumstances are, inevitably, themselves one of the features of an intellectual culture.) It is rather simply to recognize that we do customarily attribute significance to the intellectual circumstances in which individuals take shape as intellectual personalities in giving an account of them—whether in the sense of merely describing or identifying, or more radically, *accounting for* what they are and do. Such accounts characteristically run the gamut from particular associations with identifiable individuals to the vaguest notions of educational and intellectual traditions and environments. "A student of so-and-so's," "trained in Rutherford's lab," "a product of the Chicago school of sociology," "exemplifies the great tradition of German philological scholarship," "enjoys the advantages (and limitations) of the Jesuit educational tradition," "you must remember that he began as a biologist," all of these are efforts, subject to great risks, at locating individuals in intellectual species as they have emerged in the "natural selection" of the intellectual world. In effect they are a translation, into terms appropriate to the characterization of individual minds, of the diversities and pluralities which are a fact of intellectual activity.

And in these same terms one of the diversities suggested earlier emerges more clearly, since it is more easily recognizable as a differentiation of roles or functions located in individual members of the community. It is easy to see, as we have suggested earlier, that the notion of university work depends in large part upon the assumption of a kind of division of labor among its participants. No man can cultivate all fields, explore all thickets, elaborate all subject matters; and an assumption, always uneasy and frequently questioned, of organizing the work is that it can, in this sense, be compartmentalized or, in what became institutional terms, *depart*mentalized. But cutting across such a division of labor, derived from that with respect to which one carries on the work, is another, which has to do with the division of functions within the work itself, a differentiation which can be located within any department. This differentiation of functions emerges as a series of roles which individuals assume in relation to the work which is the work of the community as a whole or any part of it. Again the distinctions employed tend to be crude and unanalyzed, but that they point to genuine differences seems difficult to deny. One of them, basic to the founders' conception of institutional organization, has already been alluded to: the differentiation between the researcher, or the scholar, and the professional. Dewey's differentiation of two sorts of schools of education, one devoted to the training of teachers and one to the development of educational experimenters and investigators, is a translation, into programs of study, of a distinction which would emerge, so far as the graduates of these programs were concerned, as a difference of role or function with a distinctively different vocational structure, both of them in the same field and both ultimately related to the work of historians, sociologists, psychologists, and other investigators whose vocation is distinctively different.

Other distinctions of this kind, again complex, vague, and yet central in the self-definition of individuals and their identification by others, are not hard to find. One of them is related to a problem which concerned the new universities from the beginning: researchers and teachers, or, since in the nature of the case different functions of this sort can be assumed by the same individual, the academic as teacher and as investigator. "So and so was a great scholar, but an impossible teacher"; while "X is primarily a teacher, his scholarly work does not amount to much." And within the narrower region of scholarship or investigation, differences of intellectual role are also recognizable: "So and so is a synthesizer," or an "idea man," or a "very reliable scholar within a given framework of investigation which he did not and could not have invented." Depending upon the context and the assumptions of those who attempt such characterizations, such distinctions will issue in judgments which separate out heroes and lesser men, or even, at extremes, the elect and the condemned. "Popularizer" is hardly a term frequently now used in praise, while a "seminal mind" moves to the opposite end of the scale of judgment. And such differentiations are not immune from the influence of the other diversities we have noted. For some the archetype of scholarship and research is the careful and detailed mastery of myriads of facts, while for others elaboration of a comprehensive theoretical framework which reorients all the facts is the model of what an intellectual hero should be. It is impossible to separate estimates of the strengths and weaknesses of cultures or traditions from such differences in the ways in which knowledge is aimed at or develops.

England [wrote Max Müller in 1876] does not hold the place she ought to hold among the principal nations which supply the intellectual market of the world. It is easy . . . to cite a number of distinguished men who have been educated at Oxford and Cambridge. England will never be without men of genius. But England is deficient in those men who add atom to atom, who write short articles full of new facts, who publish in a "programme" the results of years of labour, who watch the spots of the sun till they reduce them to a system, who collate MSS., who makes indices, who are great in those little things without which there is no real greatness to be achieved in science or scholarship. Science does not grow rapidly; it grows slowly, and its real advance is marked by small "monographies" [sic] far more than by big books. Students, in England, too often try to be architects before they have been masons.[6]

Clearly this is not necessarily everyone's view of scholarly eminence or intellectual heroism, but what is significant for our present purpose is that Müller's interest is in determining what careers should be encouraged, what rewards and incentives offered to what vocations; and, of course, he is postulating a kind of education which will produce the individuals whose vocations will thus be supported. He was, after all, reviewing a book called *Essays on the Endowment of Research*. These are matters of social policy and institutional organization; but from the position of the individual, they are problems of the opportunities open to him for intellectual, scholarly, or professional functioning in the construction of a career, an occupation, a mode of personal definition of activities central to a human existence. From this point of view it is not only salaries, perquisites, prizes, and honors—jobs and careers—which are important. Prior to them, in the life of individuals, are the exhilarations and agonies, the successes and failures, inherent in scholarly and professional activity. There is always much discussion of the extent to which education should be concerned with values, but in a very simple sense any education, insofar as it enables individuals to do things they could not otherwise do, to engage in activities otherwise unavailable to them, is an enfranchisement to goods and evils, satisfactions and disappointments otherwise simply not, for a given person, existent in *his* world. The diverse roles and modes of function which are recognized in the intellectual community are, therefore, not only necessities inherent in the enterprise, functions which must be discharged if the work of the enterprise as a whole is to be carried on, they are—for individuals—specifications of kinds

6. See chap. 1, note 14.

and interrelations of goods and evils constitutive of happiness and misery. Teaching, investigating, collating manuscripts, making indices, or reconstructing physical theory are not useful motions rewarded by the pleasures purchasable by the salaries they may command or inherent in the honor consequent upon them. In fact, such other goods and utilities are a constant threat to the integrity of scholarly and professional activity; to be a threat to integrity is to be a threat to standards; to have standards is to recognize and share in goods and evils inherent in doing whatever one does well or badly.

It should not be necessary at this stage in this inquiry to point out that the satisfactions inherent in intellectual functioning are not the exclusive property of the cloistered scholar or confined to activities of "pure" research or scholarship. The expansion of the intellectual world into "all the various activities of our national life," which we traced earlier, implicates an expansion in number and kind of those whose vocational existence is profoundly structured by what they know, how they think, and by their capacity to participate actively in an expanding and changing intellectual environment. In proportion as the professions have become restructured and have been redefined by their assimilation into the world of thought, the activities of professionals are significantly altered not merely in the sense that more or different tools become available to do the same job but that the character of the function itself may be changed and the careers of individuals in those professions consequently altered. One need not postulate any radical reorientation of society to perceive that the practice of medicine, of law, of engineering, and of business have been pervasively restructured in their day to day activities by the professionalization which has overtaken them. One of the consequences, for example, has been a multiplication of specialties related to a multiplication of technologies and functions within professions; for individuals these represent choices of careers, alternative modes of defining the efforts within which the satisfactions of a professional issue. And there has emerged, necessarily, a corresponding multiplicity of standards deriving from the integrity of these functions. In this context one of the problems of standards is the constant concern to differentiate what is genuinely thoughtful from what is merely mechanical; what is techno-*logical* from what is merely technical or habitual; what is professional from what is slavishly or mechanically repetitive, unillumined by informed, thoughtful, and responsible judgment. In effect these distinctions, inadequate as they may be, are efforts to differentiate those whose participation in "the various activities of our national life" is grounded in and shares in an intellectual culture and those to whom this mode of functioning is, for whatever reason, denied.

Yet all our emphasis on vocations, professions, and roles within and informed by the world of thought runs the risk of missing what for individuals may, after all, be the most important contribution which an intellectual culture can make to their lives. It is true that a differentiation of specialties and functions—any division of labor —implicates some larger whole within which these diversities play their parts, and in this sense any individual member of the community will, if only vaguely, require some effective orientation toward that larger structure. But the conception of an intellectual culture which creates objects of new interest and satisfaction has always carried with it the notion that the enjoyment of these interests and satisfactions is not limited to those who in science, in art, or in action create or discover (invent) the objects within which they reside. In one sense, of course, the world of the arts belongs to artists, to performers, to critics, and to scholars; but in another sense the objects they create, the meanings they explore and elaborate, the values they discern belong to anyone who possesses the skills of what in the best sense should still be called the "amateur." Nor is this relationship of layman and expert or professional and amateur confinable to artistic activity. This mode of participation in the intellectual world and its satisfactions is not merely one of enjoying the fruits which fall, fully ripened, from the tree of knowledge and thought without any sense of them as fruits, that is, without any relation to the activities out of which they arose and which give them their uniquely interesting structure. We may all, on occasion, benefit from the fruits of knowledge in this latter sense, as someone totally ignorant of medical science may benefit from the drugs it has invented. But such modes of enrichment of life do not change the kind and quality of the satisfactions available to us. The notion of a "general culture" which is the fruit of education and the special possession of the cultivated mind is a far more radical conception, vague and penumbral to the world of differentiated intellectual vocations and professions as it may be. It is a mode of active participation in the life—one is almost tempted to say lives —of the mind, a mode which enriches life by transforming the world as the source and object of interest and satisfaction. "A cultivated mind," says John Stuart Mill in a justly famous passage,

—I do not mean that of a philosopher, but any mind to which the fountains of knowledge have been opened, and which has been taught, in any tolerable degree, to exercise its faculties— finds sources of inexhaustible interest in all that surrounds it; in the objects of nature, the achievements of art, the imaginations of poetry, the incidents of history, the ways of mankind, past and present, and their prospects in the future.[7]

This enrichment is clearly not the peculiar property of academics, of scholars or of professionals in any sense: on the contrary, one may well conceive that the direction of interest which is inherent in the divisions of intellectual labor we have sketched out may well inhibit or limit—and in limiting, destroy—the capacity for interest and activity which is the product of general mental cultivation.

III

It might seem that we have strayed far from our original subject and original concern. We have interpreted the "university revolution" as a sustained effort to institutionalize the enterprise of knowing—one might better say to institutionalize knowing as an enterprise, as a process in which knowledge is continually produced. But there was more to it than that, as we have seen, for it was also an attempt to institutionalize the processes in which the advances of knowledge practically impinge upon, and ultimately transform, the conditions of other, indeed of *all,* human activities and enterprises. Such transformations ultimately (as, once again, we have seen) translate into alterations of the lives of individuals—transform old activities, create new roles, enfranchise to novel sources of interest and enjoyment. Inevitably in such a context, questions concerning the relations of cognitive, thoughtful, intellectual activity to the whole range of human potentialities, functions, and satisfactions arise as questions about human beings as such, not merely as fulfilling recognizable functions in complex institutions and communities. To put it bluntly, that there must be professors and professionals if there are to be universities and the professions which emerge from the advance of knowledge may be clear, but the problem for individuals is how one relates being professor or profes-

7. John Stuart Mill, *Utilitarianism,* chap. 2. Reprinted in John Stuart Mill, *Collected Works,* vol. 10, *Essays on Ethics, Religion and Society* (Toronto and London, 1969), p. 216.

sional, with all that those functions entail for the ordering of interest, activity, career, and satisfaction, to the conditions, purposes,
and satisfactions which are human, to the activity of a life which
includes more than these things. It is, in other words, to raise the
question of the place of knowing and intellectual activity in and
among human goods.

The problem toward which this argument has been moving is
thus properly an ethical problem: ethical in a sense intended to dis-
tinguish it from social, political, or even moral, insofar as this last
word can be used to cover the whole range of problems of social
and institutional organization, policy, and action as well as the
problems of individual orientation and function. In other words, it
is a moral, but more specifically an ethical, problem. The course of
the argument has been a persistent effort to restate the conditions
and consequences of the restructuring of intellectual activity in institutional form which constituted the university idea in terms of the
organization of individual personalities, the activities these structures define, and the personal goods and evils in which they issue.
The intellectual world takes functional shape not only institutionally and socially but also in "that individual conformation in
which a vocation is forged within these dimensions of an intellectual
culture." Nor is such an indivdual conformation merely a perspec-
tive or an orientation in the sense of an understanding or a cognitive
appreciation, though it may be these things. It is a substantial ordering of competencies, functions, and activities which is expressed
in careers, purposes, and individual sources of satisfactions. It is
the stuff of which a life is made.

How does the "intellectual world" take shape in an individual
mind and character—an ethos? The normal ambiguity of such a
question serves to articulate the problem, for it might be answered
by specifying what the form or shape in question is or by an account
of the conditions and processes by which the development of such
a form is made possible, encouraged, developed, demanded, and
achieved. To the extent that the latter form of the question is answered by articulating intentionally realizable conditions and processes, it would be the statement and the solution of an educational
problem, and ultimately it is to that problem that we address our-
ourselves. But it is impossible to separate the two forms of the
question (and the answers) sharply, since (as in the case of all
"artificial" or "intended" results) means and ends mutually determine each other, and neither is invariant. Moreover, if the account

we have given of the inherent and radical pluralism of the intellectual world is sound, it would suggest that genuinely different—radically and substantially different—individual orientations should be viable within it and that any educational structure neither dogmatic or provincial must therefore at least *admit of* radically different results and probably should encourage them.

Nevertheless, it seems possible to specify some dimensions which every shape or form would have in common. One of these is *apparently* the easiest to identify. Every individual orientation within the intellectual world will have a focus in the sense generally specifiable as vocational or professional. But as we have already argued, such an orientation is not to be identified with mastery of subject matters or occupation of a job, that is, a crudely described institutional position: it is rather an ability to set up functional relations between subject matters and the purposes served in complex institutional arrangements. Secondly, every intellectual orientation, if complete, will include some effective mode of access to all the dimensions and possibilities of intellectual activity: every intellectual should have the equipment, the skills, which enfranchise him to appropriate modes of active participation in all the kinds of activities which are intellectual. For an intellectual in this sense, his profession is not a mode of limitation or imprisonment; it would rather be simply a different functional relationship to the purposes and the goods which are intellectually available. Finally, each individual orientation would be, in effect, a functional ordering of intellectual activities in relation to each other *and* in relation to other forms of human activities and purposes. It is tempting to say that every intellectual must have some sort of philosophy which could be articulated into a concept of what the intellectual world is, on what it centers, and how it is related to the whole of human activities and purposes, but it is important to recognize that, what we are concerned with here is an *ethical*—that is, functional, practical, active—form or expression of what *in another form* might be a merely conceptual ordering. Every intellectual gives the life of the mind a distinctive place, in the ordinary course of all choosing, doing, and enjoying, in his or her life as a whole, and the distinctive color or emphasis which intellectual functions and objects may or ought to give to the whole of life is not only a subject of debate among philosophers but a problem presented for practical solution to "any mind to which the fountains of knowledge have been opened, and which has been taught, to any tolerable degree, to exercise its faculties."

However, if we return to the other side of the problem—the specifically educational side—we must ask how the organization of intellectual institutions is adapted to the development of such a character, an ethos, as we have roughly outlined. In the way in which the problem has been formulated, it almost seems so broad as not to admit of or require any specific institutional location, except insofar as it can be reduced to the narrow question of professional education. After all, the acquisition of intellectual capacities is a life-long process extending throughout one's educational career, and the development of functional attitudes which amount to working assumptions as to the nature of intellectual life and as to the place in our individual lives of its activities and goods, is likely to be profoundly affected by pervasive social assumptions about such matters, which assumptions shape our attitudes from early childhood through many channels other than formal educational processes. If there is such a thing as an educational structure which effectively produces intellectuals, it would seem to be easily found in our intellectual institutions only as they are oriented toward the training of professionals, including, of course, the professional scholar or researcher. Becoming or choosing to become an intellectual in any other sense is a possibility difficult to define institutionally within our educational scheme. Anyone who asked a vocational guidance counselor for advice on options leading to "being an intellectual" would receive short shrift and probably be thought guilty of deliberate mystification.

And yet the history we have examined and the institutional consciousness which has resulted from it do not support unequivocally the view that the only way in which the problem of constructing an individual orientation toward and in the intellectual world has been and is addressed is by means calculated to produce a clearly identifiable vocational direction in students, even when vocation is thought of as including science and scholarship. It is true, as we have seen, that in very general terms the problem of giving direction to curricula in the period of intellectual expansion dominated by the university idea and university work was solved by one device or another which depended upon choosing a special direction within the maze of possibilities emerging in research, though these options might not be thought of as vocations in the sense in which that notion tends to become the equivalent of job opportunities. There seemed rather to be no way of organizing a course of study which would not be entirely random other than by some such choice— whether determined on the basis of special ability, special interest, or identifiable opportunity in the economic order. But this very general tendency was only uneasily formulated as a policy. Recognition of the complexity of the ends to be served prevented simple reduction of purpose to the acquisition of a "specialty" and often to a serious weighing of the demands of the wider context within which professional, vocational, specialized training should take place. The solutions may not have been adequate—they seldom are—but the problems were recognized, albeit in vague and shifting formulations.

In the first place, as we have also noted, part of the university idea was to raise the intellectual level of the professions by creating professional schools which were an integral part of the university, sharing in and contributing to its intellectual ambience, as some sort of guarantee that they could not degenerate into merely vocational or technical training. One of the ways in which this intellectual quality was to be strengthened and protected was by making them graduate schools—that is, by providing them with students who were adequately prepared for and would themselves demand as well as provide the intellectual sophistication adequate to the constant reconstruction of professional competence and knowledge which was to be characteristic of university work in both scholarly (scientific) and professional education. In this context it is true that the function of undergraduate, pregraduate, preprofessional, or collegiate education was in part to provide tools and competence in subject matters relevant to graduate specialization, but it was not merely that. Not only was it asserted that such studies could (and should) contribute to general culture, but—at least in some formulations—it was apparent that they should also constitute an orientation toward the intellectual world which was not reducible to the simple prerequisites of later specialization. William Rainey Harper, writing in *Harper's Weekly* in 1904 on "University Training for a Business Career," uses language weighty with difficult but penetrating distinctions.

What is it in general that the college does for the young man entering into business? Is it perhaps true that in more recent times the college has actually degraded itself in order to attract him? *The purpose of the college method is clear. It is intended primarily to develop in the man systematic habits; to give him control of his intellectual powers; to fit him in such a manner that he may be able to direct those powers successfully in any special direction.*[8]

Here clearly there is a notion of a general culture consisting in habits and disciplines rather than of a fund of general information or a nodding acquaintance with broad subject matters—in other words, a culture consisting in a *cultivation* of the mind and its powers relevant to all subject matters and "special directions."

These notions may seem incorrigibly vague—especially when set against what look like the clear demands of a special direction, whether scholarly and scientific or professional, *at any given moment.* (That those demands constantly change and change in accordance with intellectual developments that their momentary stability does not account for does not seem to provide clear curricular direction.) But also present in the revolutionary era we have been considering, and persistent throughout the developments consequent upon it, is a notion so difficult to deal with that it may sometimes be dismissed as simply a vestige of earlier preoccupations—a kind of cultural lag or merely formal homage to a dead tradition. The language in which it is couched may seem to us sexist or religious or so naively moralistic that we can hardly take it seriously. It may even seem, occasionally, anti-intellectual—an American version of the playing fields of Eton. Essentially it is the notion that education—higher education, university work, or the college method —ought to make some contribution to the formation of character, to the direction in which human powers are exerted, to social responsibility and the standards and ideals which "enrich life" not merely by providing a satisfying and remunerative vocation or new sources of enjoyment and pleasure but by providing a functional orientation of all those things toward basic purposes—human and perhaps divine. The disquiet felt and expressed at Columbia at the prospect that Columbia College might be degraded into a "mere vestibule to a professional school"[9] and the reiterated assertion that the function of the college was to "make men" rather than scholars or professionals are perhaps too easily dismissed as mere nostalgia

8. Harper, "University Training for a Business Career," as reprinted in Harper, *The Trend in Higher Education,* p. 272. (Emphasis mine.)

9. See chap. 2, note 25.

for the days when, as Flexner suggested, the function of the college was to train certain young men for the peculiar specialty of being gentlemen, and being gentlemen meant being conversant with a certain range of ideas and cultural objects.[10] (Literally conversant, one might add, since the chief function of such an education, in a jaundiced view, might seem to be the provision of a common fund of conversational references and formulae among gentlemen.) The danger inherent in the assumption of such a moral (ethical) function is that of simple reduction of the sort that Flexner's analysis suggests: a narrowly circumscribed, local, and essentially evanescent human type is identified with purposes and functions which are not exhausted or even adequately honored in it. Yet the problem seems to be persistent. Perhaps it is most obvious in the various forms of denunciation of education and college as corruptors of youth which are recurrent in this or any other society: godlessness, immorality, relativism, contempt for patriotic, "American" values, servile subservience to the work ethic—the litany of perversion is monotonously unconvincing, except to those who have no difficulty in identifying human goodness with specific loyalties, specific policy positions, and specific rituals of behavior, all mutually inconsistent. But the positive positions taken—sometimes in response to criticism—are frequently equally reductive. The notion currently prevalent that educational institutions should raise up onto the world a generation of the intellectually competent who will be fervently devoted to protecting all of us from the cynical rapaciousness of the technological culture which has largely been created by their educated predecessors is hardly more persuasive as a generous human ideal than the values against which it claims to be reacting.

It may of course be the case, as was earlier suggested, that moral and ethical attitudes (character) in this sense are formed early in life by influences much broader than formal educational institutions and that they are certainly well set before the young are subjected to the bewildering milieu of the university idea. And that idea is institutionalized in circumstances in which causalities other than intellectual development are likely to be operating. The American habit of producing a coincidence of separation of young people from family and local community and entrance into college or university may have more to do with the traditional charges of corruption (or, at least, recognizable change of habits and attitudes) than the intellectual influences they encounter in these novel en-

10. See chap. 2, note 29.

vironments. This point is worth noting, if only because it should serve to remind us that we are in search of functions which may have diverse institutional locations or which may not in fact be effectively assumed by any existing educational structure. College and university mean many different things, not only in that they discharge similar functions in widely different circumstances and modes, but also in that they discharge many different functions. An institution does not embody the university idea because it is called a university, and one need not look for "barber colleges" to find collegiate institutions which are not intended to, and from their very nature cannot, "develop in the man systematic habits," "give him control over his intellectual powers," and "fit him in such a manner that he may be able to direct those powers successfully in any special direction." It is tempting to conclude that it is more important for an institution to be clear about what it is doing in order to do it better than that it accept any particular functional role or waste whatever energies may be available in ineffectual attempts to do all things (and therefore nothing) for everybody. It is an obvious but not unimportant reflection that an efficient barber college may be a more honorable institution than a liberal arts college distinguished by incompetence and confusion of purpose. That such an institution might at the same time efficiently sustain a narrow and provincial morality is hardly reassuring.

The years which followed upon the revolutionary period in which the university idea became a central motif of the American educational system have been marked by a recognition, in many forms, of the demands presented by even these vague notions of a general culture and a moral influence or intent and by a persistent questioning of the adequacy with which these demands have been and are being satisfied in that system. Any formulation of the problems and proposals for their educational solution has always been coupled with some proposal for their institutional location—not necessarily exclusively within universities or colleges. Frequently, as we have already seen, there has been the suggestion that a given institutional structure and curricular arrangement could and should perform more than one function—thus satisfying, for example, the demands of both preprofessional education and education for general culture. Most prominent in the more recent history of higher education in America has been the notion of a general education somehow related but never reducible to a more specifically professional, preprofessional, or specialized course of studies. Characteristically this function has been variously allocated to secondary education, collegiate education, junior colleges, or some newly revised institutional structure which would give a new practical meaning to these vague institutional terms. At times the notion of a general culture has leaned in the direction of a particular body of knowledge or a way of organizing the teaching and presentation of knowledge to students; in other formulations emphasis tends to fall on the sense of culture in which it becomes the cultivation of the mind and its powers without reference to specific bodies of knowledge or information. But these are rarely exclusive, and any sophisticated formulation starting from either end usually attempts to incorporate the other. The rhetoric of these formulations is so familiar to us that it has become almost a ritualized celebration or, with a slight change of emphasis, indictment of the organizational and curricular patterns that prevail in the upper reaches of the educational system at any given moment.

In American educational discussion of these problems, no term has suffered a more curious fate than "liberal arts." At first inspection it seems to be defined largely by negation. A liberal arts college is on which does not, if only by its name, proclaim itself as directing students to any professional or vocational destination—though, of course, most such colleges emphasize, in describing themselves, not only the values we have just been discussing but their allegedly superior, or at least not inferior, facilities for preprofessional education, and almost all offer curricula which are adequate to some sort of vocational certification—one of the most common, traditionally and ironically, being in education. When the term is applied not to institutions but to studies or curricula, it has something of the same characterization by exclusion. One who studies (or, in characteristic American jargon, "does") liberal arts in college or university emerges with no readily identifiable vocational direction, though there is usually some vague range of answers to the question "What can you do with that?"—that is, what vocational directions do your studies point to or qualify for? (Frequently, of course, the answer to the question takes the form of "I can do such and such graduate work.") It might be thought that there is a notion of peculiarly liberal subject matters implicit in such studies, but it is not easy to locate. Again it seems to emerge mostly by negation— in liberal arts one studies mathematics without that basis of selection which would be provided by the necessities of any vocational orientation. In that sense the term "liberal" is not inappropriate, though still negative, since it suggests a direction of interest and choice freed from practical necessities. (Lurking in the background here may be murky notions of general culture, intellectual training, and an education for those who can afford not to concern themselves —at least momentarily—with earning a living. But there also lurks the notion of an education for the affluent and the leisured, with all the vaguely guilty connotations those terms now have.) But, positively, it seems to suggest only that the intellectual demands would be those of the subject matter as such, rather than as oriented to "practical" affairs, unless one assumes that the only demands to be satisfied are the whims of the students (or, for that matter, of the professors). Since subject matters in this sense are also in constant reconstruction—not in response to the demands of technologies and professions but rather in the continuous process of change implicit in the notion of research—and since the institutional custodians of this process for educational purposes are the graduate faculties of universities other than the professional and technological faculties, the net result for educational purposes is that "studying liberal arts" tends to mean, at some remove and subject to individual eccentricities, whatever is thought to be appropriate in the earlier stages of a course of studies which might eventuate in a somewhat old-fashioned Ph.D.

Yet this vaguely focused program does contain the results of a considerable revolution and a considerable academic controversy, for at least it amounts to an abandonment of the notion that there are subject matters or studies peculiarly appropriate to liberality. The process by which certain languages, certain literatures, certain histories, and certain scholarly traditions lost their privileged academic position as purveyors of culture and liberality would be the subject of a considerable history. It is perhaps curious that the battle against the classics was originally most noisily waged on behalf of the (natural) sciences, but that, quantitatively at least, the primary beneficiary academically may well be the range of studies vaguely comprehended under the social sciences. (Against these nouveaux riches of the academic world, the humanities, freed of classical garb and frequently highly moralized, have sometimes advanced renewed claims for attention, but it is a battle for which most of the humanistic practitioners have been ill-prepared.) But the general result of the availability for liberal purposes of all subject matters, coupled with what the late nineteenth century saw as a knowledge explosion in every existing field and many new ones, has been to produce those problems of selection and direction around which the problems of election and, later on, such reactions as "general education" have developed.

But in fact none of the dimensions of the intellectual ethos earlier outlined or their rough counterparts in the educational tradition we have just been examining would suggest that the problem of the "education of the intellectual" can be adequately stated or solved in terms of subject matters or knowledge of this or that. It is true that the tendency of educational thinking is to transform the problem in that direction. Professional competence is defined (at a given moment) by a mastery of certain bodies of knowledge and techniques. Even the equipment of the scholar or the research scientist is most easily located by pointing to such competences, though in contradiction to the traditional patterns of apprenticeship education, which amount to learning how to do research rather than coming into the possession of a fund of knowledge and information. Arguments about what constitutes a general culture run most often in terms of an acquaintance with specific traditions and some sort of acquaintanceship with certain bodies of knowledge. At an extreme, these even take the form of specific items of information or specific techniques at a level at which they can be tested for on an item by item basis. Having jettisoned classical studies as defining the cultivated man or woman, we have sought simply to substitute other studies, each of which is successively superseded in modernity and fashion by another. Even the problem of a moral direction in education frequently tends to be reduced to the teaching of some privileged subject matter which, it can be plausibly argued, effectively enables us to understand the world of knowledge and other human achievements and relate them to patterns of purpose and destiny that should enable us to serve mankind and come to some terms with ourselves and our individual aspirations. If theology no longer serves this purpose, there are available many surrogates—each offering that comprehensive view which provides a context for all the others. History in many forms, sociology, anthropology, multitudinous philosophies, life sciences,—the list is endless and frustrating. For a certain kind of scholar and professional in any field, his science or discipline *is* the way of dealing with and understanding the world and himself, including the intellectual world of his fellow scholars and his place in it. It is not surprising that efforts to communicate this vision so that it may serve for others are common. It would be surprising if they were not. What is surprising perhaps is the confusion between the specific way in which the vision was achieved and the specific way in which it functions for an individual, with its nature and function for everyone. But maybe that is not surprising either.

But in fact no sophisticated advocate of any of these solutions rests his case simply on the specific content of the subject matters he may represent. The position is seldom simply that "these truths shall make you free"; rather the claim is always present that the subject matters in question have some special relation to basic intellectual processes and problems or to the structure of the world in which they are exercised or (what ultimately may come to the same point) to the clarification of the functions they serve. It is in virtue of these qualities that these studies provide the basis for the establishment of relevancies, for intellectual creativity, for the intelligibility and consequent accessibility of intellectual and cultural objects and activities, and for effective relation of intelligence and thought to ultimate goods and purposes. In other words, they claim to provide special access to or exemplification of the functions of intelligence which enable us to construct, extend, exploit, organize and reorganize, use and enjoy the objects of understanding and intelligence which, in another guise, are subject matters, "knowns," and "knowledges." In an older terminology, they claim to be the peculiar and chosen vehicles of the liberal arts: the arts of disciplined, purposive thought; the arts of the intellectual. Such arts would not be subject matters or themselves objects of knowledge (at least not in the same sense), but they would be—perhaps in a stronger sense than President Harper intended—"systematic habits," and for an individual they would *be* "control over his intellectual powers."

Is an education grounded in a conception of liberal arts possible? Certainly it would require us to reverse our characteristic emphasis on subjects and materials—including a revision of our notions of breadth and generality—and, in consequence, to reexamine our conceptions of teaching and learning. It would require us to restructure our curricula and all the other institutionalized apparatus of education in a search for the conditions under which our intellectual resources could be refocused in the service of a process of reflective habituation. And the problem would be complicated by the radical pluralism of the intellectual world already sketched. There is not likely to be any more effective agreement as to the nature and interrelation of the liberal disciplines than there is on any other fundamental question as to the structure and function of the world of knowledge and intellect. On the other hand, as we have noted in the course of this argument, the effort is not entirely novel; perhaps all that is needed is a clarification of our intentions and our procedures. And the prize would seem to be great.

4

The Liberal Curriculum

I

The contemporary association of liberal arts with certain subject matters, certain institutions, and certain curricula is compounded with another in which they are imprecisely identified with some out-moded and incomplete forms of knowledge and certain techniques of argumentation, largely verbal in nature, characteristic of ancient and medieval political and ecclesiastical institutions. In fact, the term seems so overloaded with what, from the point of view of this essay, are inappropriate meanings that it is a good question whether it should be retained. Yet when confronted without these prejudices, in the context we have attempted to elaborate, the term itself suggests other possibilities. A moment's reflection will suggest that arts are not exhausted in specific devices—in fact it is characteristic of arts to spawn new devices and to reshape old ones in their serv-ice—or reducible to specifiable objects of knowledge. And arts are ways of functioning possessed by individuals. If the term "liberal" is to be more in this context than a vague honorific, it ought to sug-gest that intellectual ways of functioning are those of a free mind. An art, a discipline, organizes—makes purposive—an activity otherwise only accidentally, randomly effective and satisfying. In that sense arts confer control over undirected capabilities; intel-lectual arts confer control over intellectual powers; to have control over one's powers is, in one sense at least, to be free: to achieve whatever independence of circumstance and stimulus the effective exertion of our own abilities can manage.

Nevertheless, it might be argued that the term "disciplines" is preferable to "arts," if only because arts are commonly opposed to science or sciences and almost identified with the humanities in the sense in which that latter term has suffered an indefensible degradation to whatever is meant by the visual arts, the plastic arts, theater arts, and the narrowest reference of literary arts. In both associations "arts" (again quite indefensibly) tends to suggest a nonintellectual, noncognitive, and perhaps even undisciplined activity. But "disciplines" has suffered the fate of identification with subject matters (witness the commonest meaning of "interdisciplinary") and has other misleading associations, notably a tendency to emphasize "the discipline" rather than its possessor, who is likely to emerge the "disciplined." And, of course, in our permissive age to think of someone as disciplined is hardly to think of him as free, though the phrase "a disciplined intelligence" still conveys something of what we are after. In fact, however, the histories of both these terms (and of all the others to which one might turn) are so rich and their contemporary uses so diverse and unfocused (one is tempted to say undisciplined) that it is pointless to search among them for an unambiguous designation of a complex and subtle idea. Unfortunately, these confusions cannot be simply ignored, for they have direct consequences for communication within the relevant communities. A scientist confronted with the suggestion that science is a liberal art or that he can and ought to "teach science as a liberal art" (a phrase one occasionally encounters) is likely either to have his mind go blank—with the usual sense of frustration and irritation that event engenders—or to think he is being asked to give a personalized and romantic account devoid of intellectual content and interest. Conversely, the notion that the humanities can be conceived of and taught as intellectual disciplines strikes many of their devotees as a prescription for dehumanizing them. The same context, in other words, evokes on the one hand the spectre of blood without turnips and on the other turnips without blood.

But the best way to avoid misunderstandings and confusions is to say what one intends the terms one uses to mean, and despite the circularity of that process, it seems to be, improbably, possible. Let us begin then by saying that the whole trend of this argument commits us to conceiving of the intellectual world as a complex of purposeful human activities. Science, history, criticism, or educational theory are, in this form, activities in which we engage, "things we do," differentiated by the purposes they embody and the characteristic results they produce (which are in one sense the purposes they serve), by the materials we select as appropriate, and by the devices, techniques, method in which our activity forges the link between materials and (sometimes) realized purpose. Scientists, historians, critics, and educational theorists are those who are "able to do" in the sense of being able to engage in activities so differentiated and to do so knowingly or intelligently. But to do so knowingly and intelligently is to know how and to be able to formulate how. And to formulate how is to be able to say how purpose, data, techniques, and methods enter into effective relation to structure an activity and shape its product. An art, whatever else it may be, is a transmittable, formulable, intelligently purposive activity. It is in this sense that the liberal arts are arts. To add that they are intellectual arts is to say nothing more (or less) than that they are ways of thinking, differentiated forms of intellectual activity; but to say what is meant by that is possible only by specifying kinds of purposes and products, materials and procedures. It would be foolish to deny that this latter fact raises many questions.

More important for our present purpose is the observation that the liberal arts in this sense are the products of reflection upon activities in which we are already engaged. They are, to put it very directly, attempts to give some account of what we are doing and have done. It goes without saying that they are critical reflections, since we engage in reflective activity not only to see what we have done but to clarify for ourselves the conditions of doing it successfully, doing it well, doing it better. But of course much reflection is critical in another sense as well, since stepping back, so to speak, to look at what we are doing always carries with it the possibility of doing something else, if only because reflection terminates in the recognition that this activity has its special conditions and special purpose—all of which belong in and implicate a universe of purposes and their appropriate conditions. And also while such reflection is always an effort to find the specific conditions of an activity, it is not an effort to find its particular conditions. What is sought is the possibility of effective and more complete repetition; therefore what is sought is some characteristic of the activity as a *kind* of activity, one exemplified in many particular situations in each of which its conditions can be recognized and its purpose sought.

Such reflection is variously occasioned and variously justifiable. Not the least of its many occasions, however, is the situation in which we seek to share the activity with others, to reveal to them its peculiar power and satisfactions, to preserve it by initiating others into its practices: in a word, to teach it. It may be that all such teaching —from fly-fishing to laboratory science—amounts in the end merely to saying "Watch me; do what I do, and I promise you something interesting will happen," but since in large part, at least, intellectual activity cannot be directly observed, we tend to have recourse to other devices. But even more fundamental is the difficulty that mere imitation runs the serious risk of confusing the character of the activity with the way in which it is carried on by a particular person or persons—even, perhaps, a school or a tradition, whether of fly-fishing or physics. The liberating power of explicit and communicated reflection lies not only in its ability to refine and reinforce an activity by directing attention to its essential features but also in its necessary component of separating the generic conditions of the activity from its particular occasions and exemplifications. In fact, if it is in any degree complete, these two capabilities of reflection are one and the same. To recognize a personal or traditional style of fly-fishing is to face the possibility of others; to recognize that one does a certain sort of history is to recognize that history is not thereby exhausted. Of course, it is always possible that one has been fortunate enough to encounter the ideal or complete style of fly-fishing or of history, but it is a possibility to be subjected to skeptical consideration, and it can be subjected to such examination only in the context of reflection.

Reflection of this sort is a probable phase of almost any form of human activity. It has, as we have already noted, many occasions. In cognitive or thoughtful activities it may occur, with varying penetration and scope, at any stage of learning and intellectual development. In fact, it may well be argued that to the extent that learning is more than rote learning or mere assimilations of what is already known as a set of accepted facts and manipulations, some reflective insight into the nature of the activity of knowing, and therefore of learning itself, is present. In such moments, which may range all the way from learning to read to learning how to do history, learning itself becomes an enterprise which is to be conducted in a certain way, a kind of task to be more or less self-consciously addressed as such. Part of the difficulty of locating liberal education in any scheme of educational curricula or institutions derives from the

very pervasiveness of this phase of intelligent activity. The world—
and particularly the academic world—is replete with persons who
did not find out "What this or that (history or science or mathematics) is about" or "What it is *all* about" until late in their academic
and intellectual careers and who find it difficult to believe that this
phenomenon may be attributable to a defect in their educations as
much as it is to be accounted for by their individual heroism. (And,
too often, what they have found out is "What I as historian, scientist,
or mathematician am about" or simply, "What I am all about." The
force of this expression might be better conveyed by the expression
"up to," with or without the pejorative tone that phrase usually carries.) In any case, anyone who wants to think seriously about liberal
education must assume that this phase of intellectual activity can
be initiated and sustained by design, that, in fact, it can be institutionalized. This is not to claim that its occurrence for any individual can be guaranteed, that it may not and should not occur
under other circumstances and at other times, or that it is not in a
very important sense a continuous process in the life of a person in
whose life thinking has a central place. It is simply to hold that it
can and should be addressed as a problem in its own right, as an
identifiable educational task.

In fact, one of the chief reasons for insisting that the problem be
attacked in its own right is precisely that a liberal education ought
not so much to complete as to initiate a process: it should be an
effort to create a *habit* of reflection as an integral part of the life of
the mind. One might put the basic objective of liberal education very
simply by saying that it is an attempt to create a sophisticated intellectual. (That adjective should be a redundancy, but as we use
words, it is not.) But sophistication is not something that can be
taught in the sense in which we can be taught arithmetic or quantum
mechanics; it is rather a continually growing sense of command over
one's abilities and the activities which they constitute and to which
they contribute. And it is a process of growth mediated by a habit of
effective reflection on relevances and relationships among various
activities and their fruits. The purpose of a liberal education is to
stabilize that habit by providing practice and effective devices for
practice. At its best a liberal education ought to be a moment of
transformation in the life of a growing mind—a moment in which it
becomes conscious of itself and its powers as such and of the problems of assessing their fruitfulness and their limits, as well as their
relation to the human enterprises they both constitute and serve.

The stabilization of that moment of transformation as one to which the mind may fruitfully return as its powers are exercised and expanded is an essential part of the objective.

From all that has been said, it should not be too difficult to formulate the problem, however difficult it may be to solve it. *The problem of liberal education is to institutionalize those intellectual circumstances under which it is maximally probable that the reflective moment of intellectual activity will serve the purpose of permanently transforming the relationship of an individual mind to the intellectual world so that persons may become freely functioning participants in intellectual activity and autonomous members of the intellectual community.* It is possible that the statement is more formidable than the problem, but that remains to be seen.

II

Part of the difficulty of the formula just offered is that it does not seem to offer any discernible pedagogical object. It is true that the argument so far would seem to rule out the teaching of subject matters, but arts can be formulated and they can be taught. The "liberal arts" may be reflective activity, but they are also the products of that activity, and it would seem that these formulations of what we are doing when we engage in intellectual activity would form the basis of a liberal arts curriculum. For many academics and intellectuals, putting the matter this way would remove much of the mystery of the enterprise, for it would entail teaching methods, procedures, and techniques rather than subject matters, an objective of which they have at least some idea. In other words, such a curriculum would concentrate on "how to do it" or "how it is done" rather than on any specific doing or product of doing. The liberal or liberalizing components of a curriculum would be fairly easy to identify. Courses in methods or incorporating explicit discussion of methods are a feature of every existing curriculum, covering a wide spectrum of possibilities. Some of these reflective efforts are feeble indeed, as, for example, the two or three pages frequently devoted to naive descriptions of "scientific method"—usually broken down into a series of steps—in beginning textbooks of various subjects. At the other extreme, perhaps, are elaborate curricula devoted entirely to specific methodologies, techniques, for example, statistics—though frequently these are adapted for specific purposes, such as "statistics for sociologists" or "calculus for engineers." (One may note in all these latter endeavors the tendency—in itself not inappropriate—for such techniques and tools to themselves develop into subject matters.) Not infrequently the beginning student's introduction to the reflective moment of intellectual activity takes the form of a brief account—sometimes historical or quasi-historical—of the controversies concerning how a given intellectual enterprise is to be carried on. These accounts are, however, usually very brief and highly tendentious, taking the form of showing, in one way or another, how a discipline has emerged from darkness into the light in which its present protagonists bask. And, of course, there are the disciplines which, in their diverse ways, take the intellectual enterprise as their subject matter and therefore constitute an organized reflection upon it. Among these one must number philosophy (in at least some of its forms), the sociology of knowledge, intellectual and cultural history, and inquiries that because of the nature of the problem to which they are addressed, necessarily concern themselves in their own way with the forms and conditions of intellectual activity. Among these last we may number that of which this present inquiry is an example, educational theory, but there are many other candidates, including information sciences and psychology.

The difficulties in this educational situation are readily discernible. First, these elements do not constitute a curriculum, a course of studies. Largely they are elements in curricula which have other purposes and therefore strikingly different emphases. Some of them are curricula in their own right, but as such they do not do justice to the complexity of the intellectual world. One might argue that there could be exceptions to this generalization, but establishing the exceptions would require us to consider the criteria appropriate to *a* curriculum in the liberal arts. And this is the second difficulty, for the appropriate criteria are not generally met in these educational endeavors. Partly, of course, this is because those criteria are not usually explicitly elaborated, and they are usually not elaborated because the problem is not thought of as a problem to be addressed directly. If it is, the criteria are not difficult to outline.

In the first place, of course, such a curriculum must be deeply, powerfully, and persistently reflective. It goes without saying that a few pages devoted to a glib account of scientific or experimental method at the beginning of a textbook are not adequate. But their inadequacy is not simply because they do not do justice to the complexity and the variety of the activities which are scientific. They are inadequate also because they do not provide the student with ways in which he can extend or enlarge his reflection upon the enterprise which the rest of the book presumably represents. In part this is because his learning of the subject matter is usually in a presentation at a considerable remove from the processes in which the knowledge was in fact elaborated, and in part it is because little or no effort is made to make him reflect *upon* something. These two aspects of the problem are, of course, related. The synthetic (in the best sense) reorganization of material for presentation involves a transformation from the form in which it was originally elaborated, and is itself the exercise of a liberal art; but it is not that process to which the student's reflective attention is usually directed, and in any case, it is but one phase of intellectual activity. In other words, the students must be provided with stimulants to reflection, materials for reflection, and techniques of reflection. He must be engaged in the activity in a way which invites—indeed, requires—that he ask himself what is going on, and he must be provided with questions which make that a possible inquiry rather than a mere blank puzzlement or a question to be answered by a vague formula. What sort of materials in what context are adapted to provide these opportunities are questions with which the designer of a liberal curriculum must be persistently concerned.

But depth and power of reflective activity are not enough. The purpose of a liberal education is not merely to offer opportunities for reflection; it is intended also to create a habit, a stabilized attitude of reflection, so that such an activity becomes a normal, self-critical phase of the career of a developing and expanding mind. (Indeed, it is ideally itself an agency of development and expansion and therefore of liberation.) The conditions under which such habits are formed are not easy to identify, but it seems unlikely that they would be stabilized in a few moments of reflection in a course, or even in a series of courses, devoted to exploration of the problems presented by ongoing intellectual enterprises. Ideally the whole curriculum would be pervaded by a persistent shifting back and forth between doing something and thinking about doing something—or more accurately, since the doing is itself a process of thought, between thinking about something and thinking about the thinking, until the moments become so normally related that they are no longer sharply distinguished phases. This objective generates another set of educational and institutional problems, to which we shall return.

A liberal curriculum would thus be reflective and habit-forming—ethogenic. But it must also be systematic. It would be easy to derive this requirement from the hypothesis that the liberal arts are forms of intellectual activity which together constitute the intellectual world, since the notion of a "world" entails some organized and exhaustive structure of interrelated parts. But more significant educationally is the observation that the enterprise of reflection on intellectual activities, their powers and purposes, entails the discovery or construction of an intellectual world by individuals. Everyone engaged in serious thinking works upon some assumption (effective, if not conscious or explicit) as to how what he does is related to what others do or to other enterprises he might engage in. The pattern which these assumptions implicate is the intellectual world (or an individual orientation to it—for our purposes it makes no difference) for that person. Making these assumptions conscious, and their refinement and elaboration, is an integral part of the reflective process. And it is not a problem of merely speculative interest. Such assumptions express themselves in our thinking in the establishment of relevances (and irrelevances), in the pleasures and goods we expect from our various activities, and in the ways in which we estimate, profit from, and share in the work of others as well. The range and subtlety of our effective responses to objects and creations of thought are one of the measures of our intellectual sophistication and are inseparable from our practiced ability to locate and relate (by way both of distinction and assimilation) diverse inquiries and their fruits.

The burden thus placed upon a liberal curriculum is heavy, for one might seem obliged to incorporate within it what Lord Bacon called a "general and faithful perambulation of learning."[1] And the "perambulation" required cannot be a merely descriptive survey if it is to meet the standards of reflective and ethogenic involvement with subject matters in a sustained search for disciplines. To put it bluntly, a liberal curriculum would seem to require us to teach *everything* intensively and reflectively, or, at least, to *sample everything* available in the intellectual world intensively and reflectively. But a further difficulty arises immediately, for a systematic, exhaustive survey or sampling assumes some one organization of the intellectual world, a map of what Bacon elsewhere called the "in-

---

1. Francis Bacon, *Of the Proficience and Advancement of Learning Human and Divine,* book II. (It seems useless to cite any particular edition of this work or of Bacon's *Works.* The best edition, that of Ellis and Spedding, exists in several printings with different volume arrangements and differing paginations.)

tellectual globe,"[2] on which subject matters—"learnings"—can be located and which provides assurance that the world has been fully traversed. While every developed intelligence ultimately works with and within such a structure, not only is it the case that there is a plurality of ways in which such "globes" have and can be constructed and no obvious ways in which their diverse mappings can be translated into each other without distortion, but the notion of a liberal education seems to require not that such an organization be learned or assumed but that it be individually discovered. For our purposes we cannot, in other words, assume that it is there to be taught; we must assume that it is to emerge as a significant and functional expression of the activity of an individual mind.

The very real problems presented by these criteria can be seen in the checkered history of the general education movement which has played a part in American collegiate education at least since the First World War. The story of almost any of the various efforts made to restore intellectual and educational integrity to the collegiate curriculum in the name of general education would serve to exemplify the difficulties inherent in an effort to organize the intellectual world, to "cover the ground," and to have recourse to sampling when other devices fail. Daniel Bell summarizes the between-the-wars history at Columbia College with a coolness which no longer reflects the ardor with which the issues were once debated.

> The tradition of the liberal arts at Columbia was embodied in the idea of three broad courses—Contemporary Civilization, the Humanities, and the Sciences—which would be required of all students. These courses evolved slowly. Contemporary Civilization, at the start a one-year course, in 1929 became a two-year sequence, the first year dealing primarily with the intellectual traditions and institutional development of Western society, and the second year, with changing emphases, focusing on contemporary socioeconomic problems. The two-year Humanities sequence (the first year was initiated in 1937, the second in 1947) concentrated in the first year on the masterpieces of literature and philosophy, from Homer to the nineteenth century, and in the second year on the masterpieces of music and the plastic arts. Though in principle the College was committed to a parallel organization in the Sciences (successive committees called for a "specially con-

2. Francis Bacon, *Descriptio Globi Intellectualis.* (An opusculum. See note 1.)

structed and well-integrated two-year course in the natural sciences" and courses "to stress inclusive organizing principles rather than special techniques for mastering specialized subject matter"), institutional and staffing difficulties confounded the various efforts to create such general education science courses. From 1934 to 1941, a two-year course, Science A and B, was offered as an option to the specialized science courses, but this ended during the war. Since World War II the Science requirement has remained simply two years of any sciences courses, a requirement that can be fulfilled by any selective combination of two one-year or one two-year course, in any of half a dozen fields.[3]

Of course, the same problems are addressed in the "distribution requirements" (or, in the language now used at Columbia, a "remoteness requirement")[4] which provide, in one way or another, the basis for curricular construction in American colleges.

It is easy to be critical of such devices and of the unexamined assumptions they seem to represent, but it is not so easy to provide alternative and more defensible solutions to the problems they address. Even in Bell's brief description a rich assortment of distinctions begins to emerge, an assortment reflecting assumptions about the organization, the functional structure, of the intellectual world. Most of these are commonplace, but they are set to work in this tradition (and we should note that it is allegedly a tradition of the liberal arts) to organize an educational task both intellectually and institutionally. The world is divided into the humanities, the sciences (or the natural sciences), and the study of contemporary civilization, but what we are told about the latter would suggest that it is the peculiar contribution of what in other contexts might be called the social sciences. The humanities are divided, materially

3. Daniel Bell, *The Reforming of General Education: The Columbia College Experience in its National Setting* (New York: Columbia University Press, 1966), pp. 21–22.
4. The notion of remoteness is, in this context, almost a predictable device. If one assumes that there is an "intellectual globe," that in selecting a major or field of concentration one sits down somewhere upon it, and that the limitations of horizons thus imposed is undesirable, it follows almost immediately that one should seek the opposite pole to achieve the maximal expansion of horizon and experience. And, of course, on a globe any point may be a pole and will have an opposite pole, and what is an opposite pole for one point is a neighboring point for another, so that distribution is relative to where one sits. But how does one map the globe so as to determine these points? See the *Catalog of Columbia College* in any recent printing.

it would seem, into literature, music, and the plastic arts, but one might suspect that this division reflects the realities of available faculty resources and talents and the ways in which they organize themselves as much as it does any assumptions about the ultimate validity of these distinctions. Both the humanities and contemporary civilization make use of history: it is assumed that one comes to understand the contemporary by tracing intellectual traditions and institutional development and that a confrontation with master-pieces is best arranged in an order from Homer to the nineteenth century (and, presumably, from Phidias to Cezanne or, in the ab-sence of earlier masterpieces, from Josquin to Wagner or Stravin-sky.) But a systematic encounter with masterpieces suggests an educational procedure different from the examination of traditions and developments and probably reflects a distinction with respect to the nature of humanistic and social inquiry in both method and purpose. The science courses turn out not to be institutionally vi-able. We are not told how that unviability is related to the demand for "inclusive organizing principles" as opposed to "special tech-niques for mastering specialized subject matters," but in any case there is no clear suggestion here of traditions or encounters with "masterpieces."[5]

All of these distinctions—vague as they may appear in this formation—can be discussed in terms of breadth, generality, or in-clusiveness, but they have the effect of giving "breadth" a more substantial meaning, a more powerful, selective operational signifi-cance, than mere material inclusiveness or a passive "perambula-

---

5. I have not alluded here to what may be the basic set of distinctions underlying the whole scheme. The history of contemporary civilization would suggest that it is aimed at providing an orientation toward the world in which students live and its problems of institutional order, public policy, and indi-viduality. (It began, after all, as a course devoted to postwar problems in 1918). In that broad sense it is a practical orientation toward the world. It is difficult to reject the suspicion that underlying the broad triadic division here is something like the Kantian trilogy of theoretical, practical, and aesthetic. But more important than any such suggestion is the certainty I possess that it would be (perhaps violently) rejected by many who have worked in and contributed to the Columbia program over the years and that many whose view of the intellectual world is markedly different can work and have worked effectively within this scheme. It is amusing, but not very helpful, to ask what might have occurred had one suggested to a teacher in contemporary civilization about 1936 that he was engaged in an enterprise directed by the Good, the True, and the Beautiful.

tion" through the intellectual world as it is represented at any given moment by what is being thought about or taught at Columbia University, or any other "seat of learning." In other words, there is, even in this summary statement, evidence of some thought with respect to the functional architecture of the intellectual world, a distinction and interrelation of diverse enterprises with characteristic structures and purposes, presenting different educational and intellectual problems and offering different rewards. And there is also, consequently, some operative basis of selection of materials and directions of attention which amounts to a sense of priorities, for the purpose in hand, among the available pedagogical and intellectual resources. It is true that in fact what was wanted did not, in the case of the sciences, turn out to be actually available. But it is *something* to have an idea of what is wanted. It is also true that the thinking involved appears, at least in summary, to be rudimentary and vague, and certainly the functioning distinctions, even in a more subtle and articulated version, are debatable; but nevertheless they are a responsible effort to address a problem, and, by comparison, "distribution" or even "remoteness" requirements seem to be a confession of incapacity and effective irresponsibility.

But to what and to whom does this responsibility exist, on whom does it fall, and what does it require of them? In one sense the responsibility is to the intellectual enterprise, just as the responsibility of the lawyer is to the law. But just as those responsibilities implicate standards and grounds which are not exhausted in any system of statutes, constitutions, institutions, and usages, so also the responsibilities of the scholar and the intellectual are not merely conventionally definable. Any conception of the intellectual world is, or may be regarded as, merely a conception—a subjective, personal, institutional, or traditional view. But as a conception of an ordering which admits of alternative formulations, it inevitably implicates a common ground which it may or may not completely determine. It is not necessary to assume that this common ground is ontological, transcendent, or natural. What is important from the position of any member of the intellectual community is that he must assume that the world is wider than his interests and his formulations; that it embodies, in some form which philosophers may set out to explicate, purposes and standards which he seeks to realize and understand. His responsibility is not to a given conception of that world and its structure, but rather any such conception is an attempt to define and articulate those standards and that structure for him, in the interests of the enterprise in which he shares, and of his effectiveness in it.

III

Inevitably, as we have just discovered, the effort to locate a pedagogical object for a liberal education turns into a discussion of curricular and institutional procedures and structures. But it is too easy, so soon as the Pandora's box of institutional resources, curricular organization, and pedagogical devices has been opened, to forget what, in another and more fundamental sense, is the pedagogical or educational object in any educational situation—the student. Students are the object of any educational procedure in the sense that on them the curriculum and the teaching bear; they are the recipients of whatever influences educational processes exert; they are those who are to be changed and molded by their experience as students. This sense of "object" seems to carry the disturbing implication that the student is a passive recipient of whatever formative influence education may exert, manifesting himself at most by some recalcitrance. A far more important sense in which students are the object of a liberal education is that they are its purpose, its objective, not only in the sense that they are the vehicle of the purposes at which such an education is directed but in the radical sense that the purpose of a liberal education is to found, enlarge, and stabilize in individuals the capacity to have purposes, to order and discipline their purposive existence, to give them, in that fundamental sense, "control of their intellectual powers," and through those powers, control over all their abilities. It is an ancient aphorism that the liberal arts are the arts of the free man or that they are the products and the occupations of leisure and the leisured. There are important truths embodied in these sayings, but they are obscured—for us, at least—by misunderstanding and by prejudice, in fact by some of those very conditions from which the liberal arts might set us free. Not only do they seem to imply that first a man (or, of course, a woman) is free and then he (or she) acquires the liberal arts, and that leisure—a condition in which the necessities of human existence are amply provided for—somehow "produces" intellectual activity, but they are also redolent with social and economic associations. The liberal arts, in other words, are the objects and activities to which one may turn when, by fortune or design, one no longer needs to provide, for oneself, the conditions of

biological and social survival; it follows that they are the amuse-
ments of the idle and the elite. We know very well, that is, that the
Greeks (or, at least, some Greeks), having slaves to do all necessary and useful things, invented the liberal arts and transferred to
them all the social and economic prestige of the leisure class, identifying their privileges with virtue and their pleasures with a higher
good. In one form or another the myth perpetuates itself: for the
many, life, while it may not be "solitary," is "poor, nasty, brutish
and short"; for the fortunate few who land on or scramble to the
top of the heap, it is an idleness ornamented by flowers of thought
and art, by speculative inquiry, poetic ecstasies, and the self-cele-
brating enjoyments of "virtue." The scorn with which Abraham
Flexner repudiated an education directed toward the production
of "gentlemen[6] is but a pale reflection of the passions which may be
aroused by the apostles of compassion, practicality, and relevance.
It would be useless to deny that the intellectual world as it exists
in the activities of communities, institutions, and those who function in them does depend upon economic and social conditions. The
history we investigated earlier bears throughout the marks of these
necessities. John Burgess's first answer to his question, "The American University: When shall it be?" was, "It shall be when there
exists in the nation the surplus of wealth to support it," and with
respect to "where it shall be?" he argued that it would be "at or
near a center of wealth." But in his view the suitable center of
wealth would be a "center of wealth *and culture,*" and he argued
that "we certainly cannot plead poverty as a reason for deferring
the establishment of the university," observing that "the home of
the greatest universities in the world, Germany, is poor in comparison with the United States."[7] It would seem to follow that a "surplus of wealth" does not automatically produce the institutions of
an intellectual culture. Burgess thought that the American-uni-
versity-to-come would have to place its "sole reliance on private
support," and would therefore require a basic linkage to a "center
of wealth and culture."[8] But he did not argue that such institutions
could not be supported by the state (as indeed they were in Germany). Indeed, the ways in which communities have in effect set

6. See chap. 2, note 29.
7. Burgess, *The American University.* Emphasis mine. Reprinted as
Appendix I in Burgess, *Reminiscences.* The passages cited will be found in
this reprinting on pp. 349, 355, 349–50.
8. Burgess, *Reminiscences,* p. 355.

aside something of their surplus wealth for the support of those who are to become the creators and preservers of an intellectual culture are so varied as to defy easy classification. We sometimes think of Western traditions in these matters as beginning with the Greeks, but according to Aristotle[9] it was the leisure of the priestly class in Egypt which flowered originally in the mathematical and scientific traditions of which the Greeks were in part heir. The endowed leisure of Egyptian priests "produced" mathematical and astronomical inquiries which had a direct importance for the agriculture that sustained their leisure. It is a commonplace that the wealth of a technological culture such as we congratulate and commiserate ourselves on possessing depends ultimately on the "funded results" of scientific inquiry and the constant enlargement of that fund. It is less often pointed out, but equally obvious upon reflection, that the structure of our political and social institutions, our resources for enjoyment and communication, and even our most rudimentary conception of ourselves as playing a part in the world are also in the same sense the products of the labors of scholars, historians, artists, philosophers, and others the work of whose leisure has given us the language, the ideas and the objects in and through which we work out our destinies. The very terms in which the leisure class is denounced are themselves the products of leisure, and the problems of social organization and human freedom apparent in those discussions were first formulated by those very Greeks who invented the liberal arts for, in part, their more effective discussion and resolution.

These broad considerations, here too easily sketched out, may at least suggest to us why the relation between intelligence, reason, or knowledge and human freedom has been a persistent problem in the Western tradition. On the one hand, it seems obvious that the possibility of human control of human destiny depends upon insight into the conditions of human existence—not only on the conditions of mere survival but on the conditions of those aspirations which can emerge only when survival is, if only momentarily, secure, and resources are available for other activities. The arts or disciplines of intelligent insight—insight which can be stabilized and communicated—would thus seem to be the arts of free men not only in the sense that they are developed and practiced by those who are free but in the deeper sense that they are themselves constitutive of that

9. *Metaphysics* I, 1 (981b 22).

freedom. On the other hand, human history seems to disclose the impotence of intelligence as well as its power: Aristotle's remark that "reasoning by itself moves nothing"[10] suggests that the major disclosure of intelligence as to the conditions of human life is that intelligence does not exhaust them, not only because thought cannot itself furnish all the instrumentalities of action but also because thought is not itself a sufficient ground of human motivation.

The problem has its distinct, if interrelated, forms in human speculation concerning nature and the cosmos, the nature of possibilities of human communities, and the nature of human good as it may be disclosed and achieved in individual activity in those social and cosmic conditions which offer some possibility for the realization of human potentialities as such. The nature of our inquiry here does not require us to solve the problem or to adopt one of its traditional solutions. Indeed, our assumption that the intellectual world will, at any given moment, incorporate as live options a multiplicity of traditional solutions (in, of course, novel forms) forbids us to adopt one of them as basic to an inquiry into the ways in which individuals can orient themselves to that world's presented complexities and forge their distinctive identities within it. But it does require us to recognize that it is in this region and in this form —the ethical, individual form—that the problem impinges upon this inquiry. In one way or another every inquiry into the nature of a liberal education must come to terms with the problem of the relation between our intellectual life and our total lives as that presents itself as a practical problem to be given a solution in the life of every man or woman to whom fortune offers the opportunity to grapple with it.

But stated in this form the problem is vastly oversimplified. We have already argued that the university idea entailed a solution of the generic problem of the relation between intelligence and knowledge and individual and social activity in the form of a commitment to the ideals of research and democracy. The assumptions on which the advance of knowledge could be made the principle of organization of the intellectual world entailed the practical assumption that every human activity—"all the various activities of our national life"—would be subject to the influence of that advance. In other words, it rested upon the assumption that "the stabilization and enlargement of human goods in a culture and a society has as a key

10. *Nicomachean Ethics*, VI, 2 (1139a 36).

condition an intellectual culture." And, in the peculiar circumstances of American society, the transformations which knowledge and intelligence would generate in all our activities were to be democratically carried on. "Democratically" meant two things: first, the opportunity to participate in the enterprise of creating and enlarging an intellectual culture was to be open to all who could contribute to it by the standards of the enterprise itself, not by irrelevant criteria of birth, race, creed, or "alien" tradition; second, the fruits the enterprise would yield, in every sense for every activity, would be available to the society as a whole, rather than to some members of it only. In other words, universities and the intellectual community were to be the servants of the community at large. And we have seen how there emerged from this complex of ideals what might be called a notion of a democratic college—one in which one constitutive principle of one's education was the direction provided by a specific function both in the intellectual enterprise in the narrow sense and in the national life which the intellectual community attempted to assimilate through the professionalization of vocations. No doubt it is hyperbole to say that the world was to be ruled by what John Dewey called the "authority of science"[11] and that universities would produce the scientists, but it is only hyperbole.

This ideal is, like all others, subject to degradations, and the very terms in which we have stated it suggest the possibilities of corruption. In fact they are so manifold as to defy summary treatment, especially since they take different forms in different circumstances. However, the main outlines of the possibilities can certainly be sketched.

On the one hand there are the various ways in which the intellectual community—and more specifically the educational or academic community—can, under various pressures, frequently unresisted because of its own failure to understand the nature of its activity, relate itself directly and simply to the demands of the many other activities and institutions it serves, abandoning, in effect, the integrity which in the longer run makes it an independent contributor to "all the various activities of our national life." When programs of research become directly related to immediate consequences for *presently perceived* problems in those activities, when vocations or trades become professions simply by reducing them to textbooks and courses, when educational programs are evaluated—by edu-

11. See chap. 2. note 18.

cators, students, and constituencies alike—according to their direct relation to vocational opportunities and existing remunerated functions, when educational institutions are judged by the extent to which they are thought to be making contributions to the solution of social or economic problems in terms which ignore the nature of the intellectual enterprise, then the intellectual community has become the servant of the social organism of which it is a part in the same sense as any other productive enterprise. The rhetoric of service embodied in so much of the history of the modern American educational and university system—a rhetoric apparently necessary to extract from both public and private sources the resources necessary to sustain these institutions—has, in many cases, recoiled upon the intellectual and academic world with what can only be recognized, somewhat wryly, as a species of poetic justice. And, as we have seen, this way of relating the universities and the university idea to other publics and the community at large was present—and emphatically present—from the beginning. If one emphasizes the promise that the university has for improving oyster fisheries and solving the problems of municipal finance (to say nothing of the healing of the sick and discovering a "wisely diffused and invaluable concentration of sweetness"), one cannot complain if performance is judged in relation to promise.

On the other hand, a rhetoric of pure scholarship and research is no less impoverished, even if it runs in terms of a deferred or ultimate utility—a favorite device of academic apologists. It is true that knowledge may be sought and enjoyed for its own sake and that there are those who have found in contemplation (or what in literal transferral from Greek should be called the *theoretical* life) the proper end of human activity. It is also true that one can never tell what consequences for other inquiries and other activities any purely intellectual or theoretic activity may have, and that in principle any idea or any truth may have such consequences. But these distinctions simply ignore the enormous range of intellectual activity—of research and scholarship—in the social sciences and the professions which is in principle devoted to exploring ways in which human tasks are and can be carried on and human problems formulated and solved. And not the least among those problems is the problem of how scholarship—pure or applied, is to be organized and supported and how individuals may best discipline themselves in its service. That as much effort goes into the formulation of the problem and the generic conditions of its solution as into the application of such inquiries to specific problems in specific circumstances does not imply that such inquiries are merely theoretical in the strong sense of contemplative. Nor are such researches confined to those situations in which we can recognize something like a problem of action—economic, educational, social, or technological. Scholarly enterprise in the humanities, even when that region is arbitrarily delimited to the study of the arts, is, in manifold and frequently confused ways, devoted to the placement of artists, artistic objects, and arts in such contexts as will make possible the discovery, rediscovery, and reassessment of the goods they embody and shed light upon the satisfactions they offer. In this sense much, if not all, humanistic inquiry properly terminates in appreciation, not in that modern sense in which appreciation means a sympathetic sensitivity to perceived or felt elements, but in the older sense in which it means the thoughtful setting of a just value upon its object. In this form or in broader terms the humanities represent a massive preoccupation of human beings with themselves, with human powers, human achievements and human failures, human destiny. It would be strange indeed were they to be wholly indifferent to and unilluminating with respect to those purposes which are both shaped by and shape powers, and which define enterprises, constitute the standards of achievement, and lend meaning to the notion of destiny and fate. But these excursions are in danger of becoming more than parenthetical, and the whole discussion is certainly open to an objection stated earlier—namely, that it embodies the usual arrogance of academics in assuming that universities, if they do not exhaust the intellectual world, are at least the seat of whatever authority it may have, both within itself and in relation to other enterprises. (But, of course, that applies only to the "real" or "true" universities, of which there are a very small number.)

However that may be, all of these reflections are really only in aid of one point. The claim of the intellectual community to a specially authoritative, autonomous, and critical function in the human community need not rest upon the claim that it has unique objects and activities which belong to it alone, though that may indeed be the case. Rather it may be rested upon a double claim having to do with the relation of thought and intelligence to all human activities and enterprises: the claim that all of them fall within the purview of thought and intelligence and that only thought and intelligence themselves can determine the appropriate functions they have in the constitution and regulation of all our activities in their relation to each other and in relation to intellectual activity itself. This claim does not go uncontested. Since (and no doubt before) Socrates confronted the "public men," the poets, and the artisans, the architectonic function of reflective thought in the human universe (or, indeed, simply the universe) has been a question and a problem rather than a simply accepted status.[12] But it is worth noting that he did not, with respect to the poets, deny that they performed the function; his complaint was that they gave us a vision which they could not explain, certainly not even to the extent of telling us how it is an architectonic vision. (An appropriate translation of his language here might well be to say that they present a *Weltanschauung,* a world-view, and the process by which Socrates and Plato have been neutralized by transforming their philosophies into *Weltanschauungen* is an appropriate poetic revenge, carried out, of course, by poets masquerading in other guises.) Nor with respect to the artisans, the technicians, the "technologists" did he charge that they knew nothing and that what they knew did not contribute to the constitution and security of human goods. Rather he complained that each was so powerfully persuaded by the cogency and value of what he knew and could do that he was incapable of establishing that interrelation of goods and that sense of priorities among them which are essential to an organized community and a stable culture. They were, in other words, the victims of the paradox that specialization liberates by giving command over its specialty and imprisons by imposing limits upon the human capacity to function. (They have taken *their* revenge by reducing philosophy to a series of specialties and a specialty among many.) As for the "public men"—the leaders of the human community within which, of course, in another sense all human goods and enterprises are contained, he did complain that they were simply ignorant; but one might take note that in this respect they bear a curious resemblance to what he claims for himself. Is it too adventurous to suggest that what he meant was that they enjoyed an authority unsupported and unenlightened by science and that his own ignorance was that of one who finds the authority of science not in doctrine, comprehensive vision, or a multiplicity of independent competences but in inquiry and the generic capacities of disciplined thought to generate

12. What follows is, of course, based upon the *Apology,* "broadly" interpreted.

truths, interpret visions, and differentiate and interrelate competences?

But again we may have drifted from the point. For the purpose of this argument, the way in which Socrates went about stating and elaborating the powers of thought in the universe has (as, indeed, his position would seem to require) no privileged status. Those claims have been variously interpreted, variously elaborated and as variously contested. Stated in the broad terms in which they might be recognizable in many formulations, the claims of thought or intelligence to this architectonic function are not arrogant and do not commit us to a life of pure intellectual activity. In the simplest terms, reflection upon action does not substitute thought for action; rather it clarifies, stabilizes, and makes action more efficacious—in a word, more purposeful. As was suggested earlier, much humanistic inquiry (research) is grounded in the assumption that thought may disclose the conditions under which goods and satisfactions neither of or in thinking may be realized: the function of critical discourse need not be to substitute the enjoyments of thought for the satisfactions of perceiving and the joys of imagining; it may rather simply enable us to take up deliberately the position in and from which these goods may be stabilized and enlarged. The disciplines of thought are as much concerned with the tactful discrimination of the ways in which thought may thus function in relation to all our problems, activities, and satisfactions as they are with the constitution of objects and activities of which intelligence may be wholly constitutive. Its architectonic function emerges in that process of tactful discrimination—entailing the potentiality (indeed, the necessity) to discriminate and to order in relation to each other all the activities—of action, of appreciation, and of "mere" understanding—which reflection can discriminate and intelligence subserve. In these terms, no particular philosophical position is entailed, though one may be, in effect, required, and it is useless to argue that there are not significant differences among them. But one may recognize, so to speak, the terrain which all are traversing (and differently mapping).

But in the context we have tried to establish here, perhaps the best way to view these philosophies and those enterprises which lay claim (from the philosophic point of view) to be surrogates for philosophy, is as elaborations of the criteria by which the intellectual community seeks constantly to evaluate its enterprises and their effective relation to all other enterprises, to reorient its efforts, and to come to terms with the effective alternatives to its architectonic, critical function. Throughout this discussion, we have made recurrent use of John Dewey's phrase "the authority of science." As he generalized that authority and sought to heal the cultural divisions which he thought had been produced by an incoherence between the scientific world created by natural science since the seventeenth century and the world of human institutions and human goods, the outlines of such a criticism and the proposal for a massive reorientation of intellectual effort emerged in the form of a pragmatic idealism.

> There are three ways of idealizing the world. There is idealization through purely intellectual and logical processes, in which reason alone attempts to prove that the world has characters that satisfy our highest aspirations. There are, again, moments of intense emotional appreciation when, through a happy conjunction of the state of the self and of the surrounding world, the beauty and harmony of existence is disclosed in experiences which are the immediate consummation of all for which we long. Then there is the idealization through actions that are directed by thought, such as are manifested in the works of fine art and in all human relations perfected by loving care. The first path has been taken by many philosophies. The second while it lasts is the most engaging. It sets the measure of our ideas of possibilities that are to be realized by intelligent endeavour. But its objects depend upon fortune and are insecure. The third method represents the way of deliberate quest for security of the values that are enjoyed by grace in our happy moments. . . . Nature, if I may use the locution, is idealizable. It lends itself to operations by which it is perfected. The process is not a passive one. Rather nature gives, not always freely but in response to search, means and material by which the values we judge to have supreme quality may be embodied in existence. It depends upon the choice of man whether he employs what nature provides and for what ends he uses it.[13]

And were this latter alternative to be pursued, what might result?

> Needs of practical action in large and liberal social fields would give unification to our special knowledge; and the latter would give solidity and confidence to the judgment of values that control conduct. Attainment of this consensus would mean that

13. John Dewey, *The Quest for Certainty: A Study of the Relation of Knowledge and Action* (New York: Minton, Balch and Co., 1929), p. 302.

modern life reached maturity in discovering the meaning of its own intellectual movement. It would find within its own interests and activities the authoritative guidance for its own affairs which it now vainly seeks in oscillation between outworn tradition and reliance upon casual impulse.[14]

Such a program may seem to be a far cry from the idealism of Plato's Socrates, though in a Whiteheadian vein one might argue that it is simply another interpretation of the saying which enabled Socrates to reconstruct his thinking, "Reason is the disposer and the cause of all things,"[15] thus making all Western philosophy a series of footnotes to Anaxagoras. But the more important point to note about both analyses is that what is at stake in both is not merely the clarity and cogency of thought or the adequacy of a philosophical system. What is at stake, quite brutally and simply, is what sort of life one is to lead and what sort of person one is to be. For if the trend of this argument has any substance at all, the intellectual world is not a world somehow existent or subsistent over and above or distinct from the world in which we find ourselves naturally, immediately, or practically; rather it is a world in which we may live and move and have our being; it is *the* world as constituted or discovered by intellectual activity; the world in terms of which we formulate our problems, realize our purposes, and experience our satisfactions. In short, it is the world of technology and its products, of institutions and the vocations, actions and purposes they function to define, of persons, agents, responsibilities, and functions, of art and the arts, of nature and its elements and its laws and even, perhaps, of some "things" which are objects of thought alone. To be the sort of person who can and does function with respect to this world—or, if one likes, to *the* world as modified and indeed transformed by intelligence and its objects—is to be one whose sources of satisfaction, whose standards of success and failure, whose characteristic activities and problems are not merely more complex (or perhaps simpler) but different in kind and quality. It is, in other words, to function in and with respect to goods and evils enjoyed and suffered in activities and structures refined, focused, disciplined, and constituted by intelligence.

Let us pause here for purposes of illustration and clarification. We have argued again and again that in the actual working of the

14. Ibid., p. 313.
15. *Phaedo* 97C.

intellectual world, as it is carried on in the activities of individuals and groups, there is no agreement, either explicitly or in working assumption, as to the organization and structure of intelligent activity. One way in which we might be tempted to put this fact is to say that we do not talk about what we do intellectually in the same terms. And this formulation is itself reflective of our modern tendency—itself one among a set of recognizable possibilities—to discuss our basic problems and to reflect upon our activities by employing languages about languages and actions, that is, to think of the intellectual world as a world of symbols, of processes of symbolization, of meanings and the functionings of meanings in the guidance of behavior, including, of course, our behavior with respect to symbols and meanings themselves. It is probably the case that, had I chosen to discuss the problems of the liberal arts and the nature of liberal education in such terms, much would have seemed —initially, at least—much clearer to a contemporary audience. From this point of view, for example, the problems of the intellectual world are the problems which arise when we realize that we deal with—and, indeed, construct—*the* world by means of and in symbols and symbol systems, languages, in short. The key to this world is, therefore, some mastery of symbol systems and their workings—both in the sense of how we work them and how they, so to speak, work us. The search for disciplines basic to this mode of functioning is a search for the conditions which make possible the construction of different sorts of languages, the different functions of language itself, and the conditions under which languages can be effectively related to each other both in processes of communication and in systematic reorganization of symbolic structures. The argument I have made about the way in which we relate ourselves as human beings to intellectual activity would then be a statement of the various relations which individuals may have to the complex linguistic world in which they must function if they are to participate in *the* world as it is dealt with and constructed in linguistic, symbol-using activity. He who cannot participate—or whose participation is limited to a narrow range of languages (both in the sense of natural languages and in the equally, if not more, important sense of the structures of language which occur within all natural languages) and of kinds of linguistic functionings (all of which, again, occur in or are potentials of all natural languages)— is not liberally educated.

The problems of liberal education would, in such a formulation, be the problems of becoming reflectively aware of the ways in which language shapes our dealings with the world, including those other persons we encounter in it, how we use it, of what uses it admits, how these functions are related to each other, and what we may expect from the effective employment of different linguistic modes, and how we may profit from the riches they contain while learning also to cope with their constantly shifting perspectives and conceivable distortions and limitations. It might even be possible, in such a mode, to restore some meanings to the tradition in which the liberal arts have been thought of as the *artes sermocinales,* the arts of speech or discourse. It is not difficult, with the exercise of a little imagination, to perceive that all our problems of functioning in such a world are grammatical, rhetorical, and logical, and even that cultures and cultural epochs may be differentiated by their adherence to one or another of these modes of symbolic organization in some recognizable form. However that may be, the significant point is that the reflective activities in which the search for that mode of sophisticated functioning in the intellectual world which I have called the exercise of the liberal arts would be conducted by taking as the object of reflection symbolic functioning, and the terms in which the reflection would be conducted and stabilized, would be terms appropriate to that object. From this point of view the traditional disciplines would become sources which might be mined in the interest of reflection in a search for novel orientations, and the subject matters available in the curriculum would become, for these purposes, instances of the exercise of the symbol-using capacity which differentiates intelligent human functioning from other ways of relating to and dealing with the world.

But we must remind ourselves once again not only that this very general way of attempting to give some universal or comprehensive account of our intellectual situation is only one way and that it has numerous variants even "in its own terms," but also that our task here is not to give an account of the intellectual—or, as we might now see it, the human—enterprise, but rather to endeavor to see this universal situation as it is expressible in, for, and by individuals. One would hope that it would not be necessary to reiterate the point that the enterprise is shared, is social, is constitutive of and reciprocally dependent upon community and communities. The very fact that we are discussing an educational problem—a cultural, institutional problem—is proof of the necessary assumption that this is so. Individuals may have many different functional relations to

the world as constituted in and by symbolization (to stay with the
analysis we have sketched); the functional relation of the educated,
the disciplined, individual is one of those possibilities. The problem can be stated in a proportion. In a formula previously elaborated, we argued that the effort to reorganize the intellectual life
of the community which the founding of the modern university
represented rested upon the assumption that "the stabilization and
enlargement of human goods in a culture and a society has as key
condition an intellectual culture." At that point in the argument, we
could best locate individuality within the terms of a series of possible functions which that intellectual culture requires and sustains,
arguing that "the personal definition of such individuals is that individual conformation in which a vocation is forged within these
dimensions of an intellectual culture." But the problem with which
we are now concerned may be stated differently: our problem is no
longer one of individuals orienting themselves within an intellectual
culture and thus assuming some function or role within it, but rather
that of defining the conditions under which the intellectual cultivation of an individual's mind may bear to his life the same proportionate relation that the intellectual culture of a society or a community has to its "life," that is, that such cultivation may function
as a key condition for the stabilization and enlargement of human
goods as these have their being and their existence in individual
lives, personalities, and careers. Again, we argued that such a culture and such a society aimed at or endeavored to constitute "a
way of life grounded in understanding of and insight into itself and
its functions and of the world within which it flourishes and perishes." It postulated, in other words, a community which would be,
so far as that is possible, master of itself and its fate. Can we construct a proportionate relationship of intelligence and its resources
to individual circumstances and destinies? Does the development
of a cultivated mind postulate as an end some comparable mastery
of individual destiny, some sense of freedom in which it is not simply an ability to participate fruitfully in the liberation from the
trammels of circumstances and environment achieved by a society,
a culture, a community?

It may seem that the argument has advanced very little since we
first suggested that the problem of liberal education is an ethical
problem and stated that problem in the form of the question "How
does the intellectual world take shape in an individual mind and
character—an ethos?" We have tried to answer that question by

examining the consequences of thinking of the intellectual world as constituted not by knowledge but by arts, not by subject matters but by disciplines. That is, we begin this phase of the inquiry by "conceiving of the 'intellectual world' as a complex of purposeful human activities" with identifiable functional structures, structures to be identified, stabilized, and interrelated in reflective, ethogenic, and systematic encounters with them. At an earlier point in the argument we suggested that an "individual orientation would be, in effect, a functional ordering of intellectual activities in relation to each other and in relation to other forms of human activities and purposes." Since then we have raised the radical question implicit in that formulation, the question of the sense in which intellectual activity has unique claims to be constitutive of the whole structure of human activity *in so far as it is human*. In doing so, we have not argued that all human activity is or may become intellectual in the sense that all activities would be activities of mere thought—contemplative activity, in the ancient formula—but rather that the revelation in reflection of all human activities as purposive structures would bring them within the purview of intelligence. I trust the argument need not be here reiterated. In so doing, we did not commit ourselves to that position, and we have encountered great difficulties even in formulating the problems it presents without committing ourselves to *an* analysis which would entail *a* formula. But we have, in effect, argued that if there is such a possibility, it can only be evaluated and tested in a situation in which reflection of our activities is systematically habitual. That is, we have argued that the conditions to be satisfied if this is to be a possibility are those of a liberal education as we have outlined them, an education oriented toward the discovery and acquisition of the liberal arts.

Let us remind ourselves, in the interest of examining the whole course of this argument and, perhaps, extending it, that it depends ultimately on what may be, for many of us—teachers and students alike—a radical transformation in our thinking, for it requires us to think of the intellectual world as constituted not in what we know or don't know, or in what we understand more or less well, but in what we do or do not do, or do more or less well or badly, that is, in activities in which we engage. In the broadest terms, this attitude is forced upon us by the nature of the problem as we have conceived it: we have argued that we are concerned with human good and human satisfactions, with "a substantial ordering of competencies, functions, and activities which is expressed in careers, purposes, and individual sources of satisfactions—the stuff of which a life is made." Human goods (and evils) are not found in "truths" or "subject matters" by themselves, or in the mere occurrence of them as items of our experience; they are found in enterprizes, in doings, in activities. (In fact, "contemplation," in the sense in which it is a good, is the name of an activity, not of what is contemplated.) There may be a reciprocal relation between what is known and knowing and knowers, but the ethical problem requires us to approach the cognitive situation from the side of the functioning human mind. Our thesis here is that the proper ends of education, insofar as they are ethical—that is, stated in terms of the goods to which they enfranchise the individual—are to be found in the disciplined habits of thoughtful functioning which are the liberal arts. Our intellectual activity is, of course, engaged with and constitutive of objects, but it is the possibility and mode of engagement which constitutes the ethical side of that relationship.

There is what I am tempted to stigmatize as a vulgar form of this confusion between objects and activities, which may serve us at this point. We have for some time been in search of some approximation of an adequate statement of the sense in which intellectual activity may be constitutive of or a basic condition of human freedom. The reduction of the intellectual world and its members to knowledges and subject matters may have the consequence of radically circumscribing that possibility and, in effect, reducing it to an absurdity. We are all familiar with ways of talking about intellectual activity which would make a specific set of skills, a specific subject matter, or even specific "truths"—almost certain propositions—the key to all others and the sole condition under which the mind may be said to have been freed from illusion and properly oriented toward itself and its objects. In effect these positions, in their vulgar form, would have us understand that one cannot be said to be properly educated, properly aware of oneself and one's intellectual powers and their relation to human life and destiny, unless one has studied calculus, appreciated the insights of Freud, mastered the mysteries of Chomsky, understood that the earth is not at the center of the universe, or (to take an extreme case) grasped the difference between sedimentary and igneous rocks and the geological history to which they point. (Actually, of course, everyone can make his own list, and every age is likely to have its own preferred candidates.) Even this almost random list suggests a bewildering variety of dates before which it would be impossible to say that anyone had been liberally educated. Because Plato did not know calculus, because St. Thomas did not know that God is dead, because Erasmus did not understand about the ego and the id, because Descartes was unenlightened by a theory of geological and biological evolution, they were not and could not possibly be true intellectuals and, in the sense emerging in this argument, men to whom the opportunity of dealing with the world freely—autonomously—was vouchsafed. The possible ramifications of this error in less vulgar forms is an interesting problem, but what should concern us here is rather how freedom, the possibility of autonomous functioning, can be sketched out in terms which do not commit us to the mastery of certain truths or the possession of a particular metaphysics or a surrogate for metaphysics, such as, perhaps, an account of symbolic functioning.

It might be argued that the effort is unnecessary, since we may all feel competent to recognize maturity of mind and person when encountered, but perhaps some further account might be attempted. Those who have left us accounts of their intellectual and personal development are likely to be unusual people, and frequently they have been among those intellectuals who bear a special relation to the intellectual and human world—appearing as its architects rather than as its less accomplished inhabitants. Yet it is not going too far to say that the ethical problem with which we are concerned is the problem of the sense in which every mature mind is the architect of its own world. We may therefore hope to learn something from the accounts of those who have turned reflection and critical reconstruction to architectonic use, though we may not hope to emulate their heroic achievements.

Among them we may perhaps number Descartes, whose persistent habit of telling, in the service of philosophical argument, the story of his life and education offers us a relevant datum. One such account is to be found in his *Discourse on the Method of Rightly Directing One's Reason and of Seeking Truth in the Sciences*.[16] He was, he says,

> brought up on letters from my childhood; and since it was urged upon me that by means of them one could acquire clear and as-

---

16. In what follows I have used (sometimes slightly altered) the translation of the *Discours* made by Anscombe and Geach and contained in Descartes, *Philosophical Writings* (London: Nelson, 1954). All the passages quoted will be found at p. 7 *et seq.*

sured knowledge of all that is useful in life, I was extremely eager
to learn them. But as soon as I had finished the whole course of
studies at the end of which one is normally admitted among the
ranks of the learned, I completely altered my opinion. For I
found myself embarrassed by so many doubts and errors, that it
seemed to me that the only profit I had from my efforts to
acquire knowledge was the progressive discovery of my own
ignorance.

Despite this ultimate disillusionment, however, his account of the
"perambulation of learning" in which his education in "letters"
consisted is interesting for its breadth, the shrewdness of its distinctions, and the subtlety of its judgments—not always stated with
simple directness. The paragraph in which he summarizes these encounters, before elaborating them, is perhaps somewhat misleading
in its brevity and frequent acerbity, but it conveys the essential
points.

I nevertheless did not fail to esteem the exercises with which
people busy themselves in the schools. I realised that the languages we learn are necessary for the understanding of ancient
literature; that the gracefulness of the fables stimulates the mind;
that the memorable deeds related in historical works elevate it,
and help to form one's judgment if they are read with discretion;
that the reading of good books is like a conversation with the best
men of past centuries—in fact like a prepared conversation, in
which they reveal only the best of their thought; that eloquence
has points of incomparable strength and beauty; that poetry contains passages of entrancing delicacy and sweetness; that mathematics contains very subtle devices that can greatly help to gratify
our curiosity, as well as to further all the arts and lessen human
toil; that moral treatises comprise various lessons and exhortations to virtue that are highly useful; that theology teaches how
to attain heaven; that philosophy enables one to talk plausibly on
all subjects and win the admiration of people less learned than
oneself; that jurisprudence, medicine and the other sciences bring
honours and wealth to those who cultivate them; and finally that
it is well to have examined them all, however much superstition
and error they contain, so as to know their true value and avoid
being deceived.

This study of letters was followed, partly in consequence of the
deficiencies it revealed, by a resolution

not to seek after any science but what might be found within myself or in the great book of the world. So I spent the rest of my

youth in travel, in frequenting courts and armies, in mixing with people of various dispositions and ranks, in collecting a variety of experiences, in proving myself in the circumstances where fortune placed me, and in reflecting always on things as they came up, in a way which might enable me to derive some profit from them. . . . But after spending some years thus in study of the book of the world, and trying to gain experience, there came a day when I resolved to make my studies within myself, and use all my powers of mind to choose the paths I must follow.

What came of that day and some successive days of meditation is well known; but less well known, perhaps, is the way in which Descartes himself spoke of the intellectual orientation he had achieved. In some contrast to the polemical tendentiousness of his account of his education, it breathes a spirit of urbane modesty which, while it may be assumed, is none the less appropriate.

For myself, I have never presumed to think my mind in any way more perfect than ordinary men's; indeed, I have often wished I had thoughts as quick, or an imagination as clear and distinct, or a memory as ample and as readily available, as some other people. . . . But I venture to say that I think I have been very lucky; for certain paths that I have happened to follow ever since my youth have led me to considerations and maxims out of which I have formed a method; and this, I think, is a means to a gradual increase in my knowledge that will raise it little by little to the highest point allowed by the mediocrity of my mind and the brief duration of my life. . . . For I have already reaped such fruits. . . . and I conceive such hopes for the future that I venture to believe that, if there is any one among purely human occupations that has solid worth or importance, it is the one I have chosen.

All the same, it may be that I am wrong; what I take for gold and diamonds may be only a little copper and glass. . . . But I shall be delighted to show . . . what paths I have followed, and to represent my life as it were in a picture; in order that everybody may be able to judge of my methods for himself, and that my learning from common report what opinions are held of they may give a new means of self-instruction. . . .

My design, then, is not to teach here the methods everybody ought to follow in order to direct his reason rightly, but only to show how I have tried to direct my own. . . . [I] offer this work only as a history, or, if you like, a fable, in which there may perhaps be found, besides some examples that may be imitated, many others that it will be well not to follow.

If one views this picture not as a prolegomenon to the formulation of a revolutionary scientific method or specific epistemological and metaphysical position, but as an account of a mind actively related to itself, to other minds, and to what for want of a better word we must call "experience" or "the world," what emerges, I should think, is an almost palpable impression of a formidable, but not necessarily intimidating, intellectual personality. Here is a man who, in the very strongest sense, knows his own mind, not in the sense that he can state his opinions (his prejudices) with clarity and force, but in the sense that he has assessed his powers, practiced (and in practicing, examined) the possible directions of their use, determined the ways in which he intends to exert them, and effectively ordered the fruits (the satisfactions and achievements) which are opened up to him in this activity. And it would be an error to think that in encountering such a mind one does not encounter the man; *here an intellectual personality is the personality of an intellectual*. Not only would this be evident in the characteristic interests and occupations of such a man—the activities in which he finds his satisfactions—but even in the way in which he relates his intelligence and his knowledge differently to different kinds of activities and, in so doing, to other persons. In fact, the whole pattern of his life would be difficult to separate from the structure of his mind and thought. From about the age of thirty-three, Descartes lived almost entirely in seclusion, largely in order to make possible the intellectual activity which was his major preoccupation. But he was a voluminous letter writer. The preserved correspondence is a record of his thought, but it is also a record of friendships. When relations of persons are established through shared interests in scientific and philosophical investigations, the sense of a common life which results is surely no less worthy of the name of friendship than relationships grounded in the common pursuit of pleasures or of action. Thus, while Descartes lived in seclusion, he did not live in isolation; his society assembled itself around him.

Moreover, his seclusion was based on a judgment as to how best to make possible for him, with his powers and his habits of intellectual work, the kind of activity to which he wished to devote his life. That is a practical judgment, and clearly it took into account circumstances other than intellectual ones. Some further sense of how his intelligence and the discrimination he made of its functions were related to and might function in action may be derived from a remark in a letter of 1644.

> The . . . error that occurs when we believe what is not the case for a good reason—because a reputable man has said so, etc.—involves no privation, so long as we use our assurance only for regulating the actions of our lives in a matter with respect to which it is morally impossible to know better; thus it is not properly an error at all. But it would be an error if we were assured of it as we are of a truth of physics; for the testimony of a reputable man is then not sufficient.[17]

This sharp formulation of differential criteria of evidence, decision, and belief is a mark of maturity of mind, but it is also—if habitually acted upon—the ground of a distinctive pattern of life and action. But it is at this point that we may begin to have our doubts; doubts that might be stated by questioning whether maturity of mind and maturity of person or of "heart" necessarily coincide in any simple way short of some ideal which may be rarely realized. Not only are we aware that clarity of insight into the different ways in which what we believe and the grounds on which we believe it will not necessarily produce the habit of accurate and cool discrimination and action which it would seem to require of us—we may be swayed by the authority of the reputable in situations where that is not appropriate and be rashly disposed to "scientific certainty" in matters of action—but we also know that generosity, fairness, courage, integrity, and a large capacity for shrewd discrimination and shared activity in relations with others is characteristic of persons whose intellectual lives not only do not attain an intensity and range in any way comparable to that of Descartes but even to that of any tolerably educated mind. We have thus encountered once more the problems of human perfection and human freedom which have been so often debated in the terms of the relation of intelligence and action. But we have encountered them in a new and more complex form, for it is now apparent to us that there is no great gulf fixed between these two and that they profoundly modify each other not because they are conditions of different realms of human existence, which must somehow be combined, but because the common conditions of *all* human activity enter into the structure of diverse human activities in diverse ways. We may put this point in many ways. The goods, the satisfactions, which are human are to be found not

17. "Descartes to Pere Mesland (?)," in Charles Adam and Gerard Milhaud, eds., Descartes, *Correspondance* (Paris: Presses Universitaires de France, 1956), 6: 143 (*Lettre* 436).

only in the exhilarations of disciplined physical activity but in the satisfactions of disciplined thought; in both there are desire and impulse, motivation and purpose; both require niceness of perception, fertility of imagination, and insight into relevant conditions. An exploration, such as Aristotle conducts in the *Ethics,* of the range of human activities and their appropriate goods, which lies between the satisfactions consequent upon the biological necessity to nourish ourselves and the kind of rigorous intensity of thought which Descartes records in his *Meditations,* is not a journey in which good and evil, joy and sorrow, and "life" are progressively left behind in order to enter a realm occupied only by some ghostly ballet of bloodless categories. And the pattern of a human life which consists in the effective realization for an individual of the whole spectrum of human purposes and human goods, admitting of almost innumerable variations of actual ordering, *is* character, person, individuality. "Maturity," or "individuality," in a strong sense is simply the name we give to that condition in which a person has given an order to the range of human functionings, an order which gives to his relations with the world of other persons, of objects of desire and interest, of experience, a distinctive and sustainable structure of purposive functioning. In thus ordering his activity, he will have ordered purposes, or, to use somewhat Kantian language, he will have created for himself an identifiable functional purposiveness. What we encounter in such a mind and person is that purposiveness; to know one's own mind in this sense is to know "what one is about," not primarily in the sense of knowing oneself as a describable object, but knowing what it is to "go about *my* business." Such an individual is autonomous not because he can supply all the conditions of his activity from his own resources but because resources become resources and are determinately employed in their relation to *his* purposiveness—that is, to himself.

All that we have asserted in this long and rather tortuous argument could perhaps have been more simply elicited by recognizing from the beginning that there might be an educational enterprise devoted to the exploration of the world of thought and intelligence as a world of human goods and human purposes. The difficulties of the argument have derived mainly from a double way in which intelligence is related to the whole range of human activities which is structured by purposes and in which goods are realized. With respect to some human activities, intelligence is constitutive only in the sense that without it activity is mechanical and only externally related to other activities. With respect to others intelligence is constitutive in the sense that they are the activity of intelligence itself. We may leave to philosophers the further formulation and clarification, in whatever terms they may find appropriate, of these distinctions and the interrelation of human goods and activities they seem to postulate; for the present, however, we may observe that our criteria for a liberal curriculum require, in the light of these considerations, some amendment. A liberal curriculum must be not only reflective, systematic, and ethogenic but also what we may call—for want of a better word—*teleological*. That is, reflection must systematically take account of the purposive character of intellectual activity.

There are serious dangers here. They are the dangers of moralizing, which we may more precisely define as the vices of dislocation and reduction. Dislocation occurs when goods and values are detached from the structures of activity in which they are realized and which give them the identity they have, so that they float before us as undeniably worthy aspirations to which we cannot and need not have any effective, practical relationship. There is thus generated a comforting sense of being on the side of the angels, without any sense of what angelic activity might consist in. Reduction occurs when one good or value is found sufficient to account for all—with the consequences (given the reciprocal relationship of values and activities) that all activity is reduced to one activity. Generally, this phenomenon occurs in one of two ways. Either there is a practical restriction of human activity to one possibility, or a complex of activities focused upon a particular problem which becomes *the* problem to the exclusion of all others. Both are fairly easy to recognize. Hegel remarked that "to him who looks rationally at the world, the world looks rationally back"; reduction of the first sort occurs whenever "rationally" is restricted to some one of its possibilities. To him who looks scientifically at the world, the world looks scientifically back. From this it is only a step to: "to him who looks chemically at the world, the world looks chemically back." And, of course, the sciences are not peculiarly guilty in this respect; it is also the case that to him who looks historically or geographically at the world, the world looks back accordingly. Reduction in the other sense is sometimes more subtle in structure, since it frequently takes the form of identifying some problem or crisis or dilemma of culture, of civilization, or of epoch for the resolution of which all—or at least many—disciplines are relevant. It should not be necessary

to sketch out some of these possibilities—but in a moment of perhaps self-criticism we may perhaps wonder whether individuality,
as we have discussed it here, is not such a reduction. But what is the
remedy for such evils? Only systematic, ethogenic, teleological
reflection.

Whatever may come of that doubt, it is important to recognize
that individuality, as we have discussed it, is an achievement, not a
gift of nature or a status automatically conferred by our numerical
identity as particular human organisms. And it is an achievement
without specific content or shape. To return to our basic concerns,
liberal education is not successful because it produces geniuses,
Cartesians, or intellectuals who live in seclusion in Holland or, for
that matter, in Princeton. Nor is individuality or autonomy something conferred by an undergraduate degree or probably achievable
in any specifable number of years of institutionalized intellectual
life. We must remind ourselves that we seek in a liberal curriculum
only the institutionalization "of those intellectual circumstances
under which it is *maximally probably* that the reflective moment of
intellectual activity will serve the purpose of permanently transforming the relationship of an individual mind to the intellecual
world so that persons *may become* freely functioning participants
in intellectual activity and autonomous members of the intellectual
community." A liberal curriculum is at best the initiation in a
process, a development, not itself the achievement of the end to
which it is directed.

But one further note. The trend of this argument, with all its
dubieties, might suggest that we have too conservatively formulated
our aim—perhaps we should have said that it was the "permanent
transformation of the relationship of an individual mind to *the
world* so that persons may become freely functioning participants
in *human* activity and autonomous members of the *human* community." But perhaps we need not worry too much about it, since
one thing at least may be clear: the more restricted formulation is a
condition of the larger one. Even if we reduce intellectual activity
and the intellectual community in the narrower sense to some
merely useful appendage to some other community and some other
activity, without it the human world would be remarkably impoverished.

5

Institutionalizing

I

Whatever may be thought of the speculations into which this inquiry has led us, we must now recall that we have described the problem of liberal education as a problem of *institutionalizing*. In the most general terms one might say that the founding or the changing of institutions is a search for available resources and modes of organizing them into relatively stable patterns of functioning such that some human purpose may plausibly be served. The resources in question are of two very general sorts. There are human beings with capabilities and purposes of their own, variously related and sharable, and there are other resources—as, for example, libraries and laboratories—which are necessary if the activities defined by human capabilities and purposes are to be possible at all, minimally or maximally effective, and invested with any reasonable prospect of continuity and development. And, of course, some problems which enter into the structure of all human enterprises are present: problems of leadership, of communication, of organized decision-making, of priorities, and so on. There is need of a term to describe this latter dimension of any such problem, since the word "politics" (an obvious candidate) tends to be restricted in two different ways. First, it is limited (with good etymological justification) to this dimension of the problem of organizing the whole community within which many other enterprises are carried on, so that it needs an adjective to be specified to any one of them—

as in *"academic* politics." Second, it has become a generally pejorative term singling out those ways of exercising leadership, communicating in the interest of action, making decisions, and setting
priorities which do not require any consideration of the nature and
purpose of the enterprise being conducted. It is therefore fashion-
able—perhaps particularly among academics—to profess, at least,
contempt for politics. While such an attitude may be based on a
genuine distaste for "wheeling and dealing" or "doing jobs," it is all
too frequently an expression of incompetence, an avoidance of responsibility in the interest of other activity (sometimes scholarship,
sometimes less lofty preoccupations), or the result of a stubborn
narrowness of conviction as to how a given enterprise is to be carried on, an attitude incompatible with any effective sharing of the
enterprise with others on terms of practical equality. In any case,
the business of liberal education is not for those who are unwilling
to dirty their hands in politics.

But more significant for the purpose in hand—that is, saying
something useful about institutionalizing—is that in the nature of
the case institutionalizing is a highly circumstantial activity, as is,
indeed, any problem of action. One would hope that it is not necessary to prove or to elaborate upon this truth. But it is worthy of note
that it bears upon the meaning of "available resources and modes
of organizing them" in two quite distinctly different but interrelated
ways. One has to do with a question which can be described as
economic in the sense in which economics has sometimes been
thought of as an analysis of economizing—that is, the allocation of
limited resources among competing activities. This is a question of
whether resources are available at all or whether they are adequately
available. One must face the fact that the function and the purpose
which are liberal education are always in a competitive situation in
this sense. Educational or intellectual institutions do many things,
and they allocate their resources accordingly; it is redundant to
point out that these resources are not unlimited. The shape of some
of the problems we have encountered in the course of this inquiry
may be regarded as partially the consequence of this problem, or
recalcitrance of availability. The persistent effort to separate sharply
university and collegiate functions, the suggestion (by Harper
among others) that institutions such as colleges should "individual-
ize" or specialize by limiting themselves to a single function or a
specific form of one function, the continuing argument as to which
institutional system (as, for example, secondary school or college)

should be responsible for what—all of these are in part efforts to shift the burden of work from one set of resources to another in a situation in which availabilities are limited. (As we noted earlier, perhaps the most important of these consequences has been the repeated suggestion that a curriculum could serve simultaneously the purposes of general culture and preprofessional training.) And, of course, in large part this problem is one of what sources of support —in the broadest sense of economic availability—are thought to be tappable for a given enterprise in a given set of circumstances.

But an equally serious problem is presented by the other sense of circumstantial availability—not a question of whether, for whom, from whom, and on what scale resources are available but rather of what is actually available, that is, of the form or shape in which resources present themselves to be employed. In any process of creation or functional reorganization (that is, reorganization in the interest of a novel or clarified function) only God, if he (or she) is fortunate enough to be divine according to the right theological tradition, creates *ex nihilo* or from prime matter—a pure, entirely undifferentiated potentiality. The rest of us (including the gods of many less radical theological traditions) must work always with something already formed, already functional, already shaped. Pharaoh, in some unaccustomed fit of rationality, may decree that the Israelites receive an appropriate allocation of clay and of straw. But what kind of clay and what kind of straw? While one cannot make bricks without straw, it does not follow that all sorts of bricks, or that good bricks of any sort, can be made with this straw and this clay. And if the workers have cultural habits which forbid the division of labor as between, say, mixing and shaping, the difficulties of productivity are further compounded. The proximate resources of any educational enterprise include most prominently the human resources of teachers and students; in comparison, bricks and straw are prime matter. One is never dealing with teachers and students; one always deals with scholars with specific capacities (and incapacities), specific habits and expectations concerning the routines of teaching, of associated decision-making, of examination and certification, of the organization of their work with others, and even of the rewards (financial and other) which should properly accrue in their careers. And, mutatis mutandis, as we are sometimes likely to forget, the same differentiae apply to students—not only in colleges and universities but in kindergarten and first grade. And these available capacities vary with traditions, kinds of institutions, frequently significantly within institutions, and from individual institution to individual institution. Consequently, to say that teaching time or teaching resources are available because a budget has been supplied for them is to say little of any importance as to what is in fact made available in relation to the function to be performed.

The consequence of all this—apart from the apparent impossibility of saying anything useful about institutionalizing apart from a specific set of circumstances—is that any given set of educational practices or devices cannot be simply transferred from one set of circumstances to another without effectively changing its meaning and functional efficacy. Yet much of our practice in effect denies this truth, and every educational movement tends to fall into the traps it sets for the unwary, for the tendency of such movements is to identify purposes and functions with specific devices, specific modes of organization, and even, sometimes, specific materials. Nothing is in fact more destructive of a genuine educational idea than its reduction to such devices and their replication in ostensible forms in diverse circumstances. That is why the basic strategy of this inquiry has been to search for the functions and purposes which specific modes of organization and educational devices serve and make useful, even to the extent of examining the history of institutions in terms which give priority to these dimensions of institutional order and change. Indeed, for the properly political mind —we should probably say the institutional and institutionalizing mind—problems of action are interesting *because* they are new in every set of circumstances, precisely because, in other words, they are always different and yet, as problems of recovering and reenacting similar functions in diverse circumstances, always the same. Experience, whether in the form of history or some other structure, is a source of discouragement insofar as it seems to offer no clearly replicable solutions to our problems—it seems to say rather helplessly, "Do the best you can." On the other hand, it is also a record of human ingenuity and inventiveness from which we may intelligently profit, and the persistence of the problems to which we address ourselves is some assurance that they are not merely the product of our unique circumstances.

Nevertheless there is a middle ground for thought between the search for functions and purposes, including the articulation of criteria which would have different significance in every particular set of circumstances, and the consideration, by specific individuals confronting particular circumstances, of how these functions are to be organized, these purposes sought, and these criteria met. In large part the existence of this middle ground is the consequence of the fact that resources (particularly human resources) are always presented in some previously organized form and that these forms are the consequences of existing institutions or, if one prefers this language, of cultural and social circumstances. From this point of view, what are institutions and cultures but ways of shaping human beings into more or less recognizable functional entities with similar structures of capability and expectation, and a relatively limited repertory of diversity in these respects? Plato argued in the *Republic*[1] that the quickest way to establish a totally novel institutional order would be to remove everybody over the age of ten, thus permitting innovators to shape their human resources to fit the new society. (One may argue about the age, I suppose, and Plato himself was aware that this left the genetic problem untouched, a circumstance in which he found the ultimate undoing of the new community.) But short of such a possibility of wiping the slate clean, we are not normally confronted in any actual situation with an absolute chaos any more than with a completely realized and therefore utterly recalcitrant order. It is therefore always possible to attempt, at least, some diagnosis of the most relevant circumstances which are likely to be, in a particularized form, of course, ingredients of any problem of institutionalizing in an identifiable culture, society, or institutional organization. In other words, the continuities of institutions and the habits they engender in individuals lend to the theater of action a relative stability without which any calculations of means and ends, resources and purposes would be almost impossible. But, of course, it is only a calculation and it rests upon judgments, all of which are fallible. We deal only in tendencies and probabilities, estimates and trends, and we run the serious risk of confounding our general diagnosis and our general calculations and deliberations with specific answers to specific problems. In educational matters, there are no recipes; there are only general directions of possible solutions for problems based on an informed and experienced estimate of probable availabilities, opportunities, and obstacles in a set of circumstances given order and continuity by existing and antecedent institutions. In a word, there are strategies.

The proximate world within which the enterprise of liberal education must be organized is the academic world as we know it, and

1. *Republic*, VII, 540E *et seq* and 545E *et seq*.

therefore it is appropriate to ask what strategic problems it presents to us. It is tempting at first sight to think of moving outside of the existing institutions to found a new kind of institution not subject to the constraints of those that presently exist. This is a strategy which has been tried and no doubt will be tried again.[2] But it is an illusion to think that we thereby achieve the Platonic freedom from circumstantial determination alluded to above. The students and teachers who will enter into association in this new institution will all (probably) be more than ten years old, and therefore they will all in one way or another be products of the institutions which we are seeking to supersede. It may be that they will not all be disillusioned products, misfits or rejects, who define themselves by negation only, but in any case it is a strategy which requires the exercise of great skill in leadership and governance if such an institution is not to degenerate into a celebration of otherwise purposeless dissent. But more important is the point that even in such a situation we cannot completely escape from ourselves and the influences that have shaped us. The more difficult questions therefore arise when we consider how we are to use our existing habits and capabilities in shaping new or different ones—and that is a problem which working within and working without existing arrangements have in common.

It was partly in the interest of attacking strategic problems that an inquiry into the origins of our present institutions of higher education was undertaken. And now that we have arrived—partly by the aid of that examination—at some conception of the function and purposes which we call liberal education, it behooves us to consider those institutions, from the point of view of institutionalizing—within, around, through, or with them—that function. At first sight it would seem that the circumstances are nearly ideal, for, without entering into historical controversy, it would seem difficult to find a situation in which intellectual activity, in all its varied forms, is more fully represented or intensively pursued than in the modern large university. Here we may have recourse to our earlier discussion of the diversities which are encountered in them (and were in fact deliberately sought and cultivated by the founders)—

2. An important variant of this strategy is to move outside existing structures *within* institutions—that is, to found something alongside or as an alternative to other institutional parts. The perils of experimental colleges and other such arrangements are fairly obvious, but there is much to be said for this device.

diversity of inquiries, researches, and subject matters, functional diversity of intellectual presuppositions as to the nature of the activity, diversity of roles and functions within enterprises, and diversity of relation of intellectual activity to other activities. And we should take note that what makes a university large is precisely this diversity, this complexity of activity—not number of students, campus acreage, numbers of faculty, or size of budget. But, in any case, the presence of these diversities in intensely active form would seem to offer the most auspicious circumstances in which a growing mind might be engaged by a relatively simple process of selection in the kind of activity which we have argued is suited to developing "systematic habits" conferring "control over intellectual powers," and fitting persons in such a manner as may enable them to "direct those powers successfully in any special direction."[3]

Alas, it is not so, or not simply so; the reason (and it is a reason, not a cause, or at least that kind of cause which is a reason) is not far too seek. This whole complex of activity, in all its diversity, is oriented toward and takes its organic structure from the advancement of knowledge, or from what, in the operative terms appropriate for institutional functioning, is called productive research. It is true, as we have seen, that the enterprise is also profoundly affected by the sense that advancing knowledge may and indeed must serve purposes not easily identified as merely cognitive or intellectual, but the proximate end for which the institutions themselves are organized and which they serve is the production of the knowledge which may serve such other functions. It is not simply that we assume that if "knowledge grows from more to more," the enrichment of human life may be allowed to take care of itself, but rather that what may be needed in addition is more knowledge, knowledge of how knowledge enriches life. But from our present vantage point it becomes apparent that the entire thesis of this argument has been that there is no simple equivalence between the advancement of knowledge and the growth of the mind, whether of the community as a whole or—what is our special concern—of the individual. (A striking way of making the point in a somewhat extreme fashion would be to say that it is not surprising that searches for knowledge of how knowledge enriches life frequently emerge with the discovery that it does not. After all, that is what is meant—in, I hope, a carefully guarded

3. William Rainey Harper, "University Training," p. 272.

sense—by saying that a liberal curriculum is teleological, namely, that it is a constant search for those functional intellectual conditions under which knowledge may enrich life.)

The result—again in its massive impact—is that to the extent that intellectual institutions are efficiently purposive in the service of the end to which they are dedicated they seem to be designed to exclude the function, the purpose, which we have argued is liberal education. The simple way of identifying this powerful tendency is to point out that the whole complex of resources and activities which is a university relentlessly organizes itself and defines its parts in terms of, by reference to, and in the service of elaborating subject matters, knowledge, facts and truths. The faculties which, in their own view, at least, continue to constitute the core of the university (in the terminology with which our forebears were familiar, the "philosophical faculty," or what John Burgess called "the life and glory of the university" and "the foundation of everything further"[4] distribute themselves into what look like subject matter areas. Even in those parts of the university in which the very names would seem to suggest activities or functions rather than knowledges and subject matters, parts such as business or law or even engineering, there is an unremitting effort to define these activities as themselves subject matter or by assembling the subject matters which are thought to be instrumental to the activity. In certain fields the results are almost comic in their general aspect. One can study, in a large university, almost any history one likes, provided one identifies the object as one of those subject matters which have been or are elaborated in historical inquiry. But it is very difficult to study *history*. And since the inquiries or subject matters are infinite in principle, so is the size of the department of history. And, of course, it is not just the curriculum, in the sense of what one learns or studies, that is thus affected; the activities of teaching, the expectations of students, the capabilities of members of the community (scholars, teachers, students, *et al.*) and the organization, allocation, and use of resources such as libraries and laboratories are described, identified, and evaluated in reference to and persistently adapted to the demands of inquiries which are thought of in terms of the results of the activity in which they function— contributions to, development of, or elaborations of fields or subject matters.

4. See chap. 2, note 15.

The problems presented by this picture are sometimes discussed as if they were problems of teaching and research—activities which are opposed to each other either because it is thought that the allocation of resources between them is disproportionately weighted toward research or because it is argued that the competences involved are different and that academics are inadequately trained as teachers, however well equipped they may be for research. But in these terms, without further analysis, the problem is oversimplified. With respect to the allocation of resources, it is not obvious that if all research were stopped tomorrow and all faculty resources made available for teaching that any significant progress would be made toward liberal education, even supposing that only the good teachers were kept on, or that everybody were to be retrained as a teacher. The question really is one of what the function of teaching is thought to be. There are many good teachers whose excellence (and it is indeed an excellence and a relatively rare one) consists in their capacity to enable students to assimilate with maximum efficiency, minimum pain, and even considerable enjoyment a large body of material. But their devices and their imaginative ingenuity are not therefore adapted to the systematic stimulation of that reflective activity which is essential to a liberal curriculum. And the same may be said, in proportionate terms, of students. We referred earlier to the expectations of faculty and students. "Expectations" incorporates a significant ambiguity. Students work on assumptions both as to what is expected of them and as to what they may legitimately expect to gain. When they think they are expected to learn something (whether chemistry or the history of the Hapsburg empire), they will function accordingly, and they will think they have succeeded when they know chemistry or Hapsburg history. There are excellent teachers who systematically inculcate and satisfy such expectations.

But this vision of the university is distorted. So far we have stated the facts in terms which structure them as dangers, impediments, or difficulties. A different view emerges if we treat them as resources and opportunities—a transformation which occurs simply by asking how one can take an effective initiative in the use of what is present in the institution. After all, the diversity of activity and function is there, and it is represented not only in the fruits of what is done, but also in the doing of it and in the habits, activities, and opinions of those who carry it on. The problem then is how to bring all of these elements into some relationship that will focus

attention on them in their character as elements of activities. And
we should observe in this connection, as a first step on the road to
an initial formulation, that there is, in fact, a strong sense in the
university of fields or inquiries as alternative modes of thought, as
representing choices which actually structure what is done and
what emerges from the doing. There is even a considerable discussion of these problems—at many levels of generality and at
different degrees of intensity in different fields at different times.
Interpreted as changes of fashion or destructive controversy, such
discussions are appropriate objects of cynicism and partisan pas-
sion; but as signs of the possibility of redefining fields and reorganizing the structure of inquiries with consequent differences in what
they may be expected to yield, they are opportunities for bringing
into effective focus questions concerning the powers of thought, of
inquiry, and of those knowledges which are its fruits. In other words,
the intellectual community is—in effect and in many guises—constantly engaged in reorganizing itself, in reassessing the special directions in which it may exert its powers, and consequently in restructuring its work. There may even lurk somewhere in the minds
of some academicians the suspicion that one criterion of a good
university is the extent to which alternatives are effectively present
in it, are recognized, discussed, and assessed by standards which are
themselves under continuing discussion. If the undergraduate curriculum (or some undergraduate curricula), the college, or the liberal curriculum as a function in the university is taken as a place in
which this dimension of university work is to be focused, exploited, and organized, there would be, not a general relationship of
competition for resources, but a genuine coincidence of functions
in which neither need profit or suffer from the other. And there
might even emerge an actual perception of the university as a whole
or of the whole university as present in the undergraduate or collegiate function, a sense not reducible to the presence there, as
things to be studied, of all subject matters. Another way of putting
the matter would be recur to something which has been asserted
again and again in this inquiry, namely, that the reflective moment
in thought is not something alien, strange, or forced. It is simply
what happens when we think about what we are doing. True, we
are inclined to *say* that we are forced or required to think about
what we are doing—a locution which derives from the obvious
fact that something has gone wrong in the doing. "What is the
sense," asked Whitehead in attempting to define one such mo-

ment, "of talking about a mechanical explanation when you do not know what you mean by mechanics?"[5] That something has gone wrong and that we are likely to perceive it by the recalcitrance of what we are attempting to explain is easy enough to see; what is somewhat more subtle, but none the less obvious "upon reflection," is that that recalcitrance which forces reflection upon us is a phenomenon which as a felt event can only occur in a purposive activity—in this case, an activity of explanation. It would seem to follow, as Whitehead suggests, that the recalcitrance or the force is to be attributed as much to the explanatory activity as to what we are attempting to explain. In this sense we force reflection upon ourselves by a commitment to purposive activity. We might never encounter such difficulties. That is, to recur to the words of John Dewey, our experience might consist entirely of moments in which "through a happy conjunction of the state of the self and of the surrounding world, the beauty and harmony of existence is disclosed." In that case there would be no need for what he called "deliberate quest for security of the values that are enjoyed by grace in our happy moments."[6] But while we await the kingdom of grace, reflection is not only inevitable but natural. The search for a liberal curriculum is the unremitting effort to bring into the focus of attention the deliberative moment of the quest for security of activity and of good.

But to bring it into focus is not, should not be, to isolate it from the enterprises in which it is a function. To do so would be to commit an error opposite to but no less serious than that of isolating the results of inquiry from the processes in which they originate and the reflection which assesses their intellectual status. Anyone who has ever engaged in attempting to construct and actually institute a curriculum of the sort we are discussing is familiar with the charge that it is not devoted to teaching science (or history or mathematics) but to teaching *about* science, or, in another form, that it substitutes the philosophy of science, or scientific method, for science, or, most simply, that it reduces the whole curriculum to the teaching of philosophy. One may observe in this concern and its formulations two relevant considerations. First, it represents the common assumption that to change a curriculum is to substitute

5. Alfred North Whitehead, *Science and the Modern World* (New York, 1926), p. 24.

6. See chap. 4, note 13.

one subject matter for another: the philosophy of science for science, historiography for history, and so on. Secondly, so far as the intention and effect of innovation *is* to substitute one subject matter for another or to isolate the reflective moment of thought from its other moments, it is a legitimate concern and a sound objection. If, as we have argued, the purpose of a liberal education is to initiate reflection on the form, conditions, and consequent fruits of enterprises of thought, it cannot make sense to substitute, in the name of stimulating and encouraging the reflective moment of one enterprise, another enterprise. What complicates the problem, of course, is that in reflection we are trying to stabilize and identify the enterprise itself—a situation in which its apparently solid and given character is necessarily lost. No formula for this activity can be totally without possibilities of misdirection, but if we think of the reflective moment not as a moment for teaching philosophy but as a moment of philosophizing, and practically mean by "philosophizing" what we do when we are engaged in trying to locate, identify, and organize for ourselves an activity in which we are already engaged, some of the difficulties both of communication and practice may be avoided.

To put the matter simply, reflection which is to be fruitful is not blank introspection; it is reflection upon something—upon an activity in which we are engaged with something. A curriculum, a course of studies, must therefore provide that with which we are to be engaged, engage us in it, and so organize that engagement that it maximizes the opportunities and occasions for reflection. Ideally every element in the curriculum would carry all the functions suggested in that formula, but whether that can be achieved in any actual circumstances is not something which can be predetermined. In large part the problems of designing a curriculum (as opposed, for instance, to designing elements of it) is determined by the circumstantial availabilities in this sense. A simple example may suffice to make the general point. If there are many histories being taught—and well taught in the sense we discussed earlier—the strategic problem of designing a curriculum may take the form of asking how the students' effective engagement in such teaching and learning with history can be effectively exploited, in a curricular context which courses in histories would provide, for purposes of reflection. That is not the same thing as completely changing the teaching of history. If devices (and they must be curricular devices) can be invented to attack the educational problem presented in this form, the result will be that the efficiency of the teaching of histories will serve, without distortion or strain, the function of liberal education.

There are a number of other basic considerations which must be kept in mind in any process of devising educational strategies, that is (as we may now reformulate the problem), in locating relevant resources and organizing them effectively. (I hesitate to call these considerations truths or facts, since functionally they are rather tools for solving a certain kind of problem than assertions about the world.) Among these other considerations one might put first that a curriculum (and one must include in that word all the dimensions of academic or educational functioning, including materials, teachers, courses, examinations and other evaluative techniques, and so on) is, in a very strong sense, that which teaches or educates. It would be foolish to deny that teachers also teach and educate, but the structure within which they work is, from the point of view of any actual sequence of teaching activity on the part of one person, so powerful an influence that it deserves a most serious consideration in its own right. (I am inclined to think that this would be the case even though there were but one teacher in the curriculum, but that is a practically moot point.) From the point of view of the curricular architect, it must be assumed that it is the curriculum that teaches. This is a matter of supreme practical importance, partly because it is a dogma common among many academics that curriculum is of little importance and that teaching is, or that teachers are. (When my colleagues tell me that curriculum is not something they are interested in or that there is too much talk about it, I cannot but wonder whether they are simply asserting that they have not thought about education, that they are but humble workers in the vineyard who rely on others to design and direct the enterprise, or that somehow they think they *are* the curriculum. But there are many other possibilities.) If one thinks, for instance, of the curriculum as it bears upon and creates student expectations, in the double sense mentioned earlier, it should be clear that it teaches—that is, creates and orders those expectations—not only by the selection of certain elements rather than others, but by the juxtaposition of those elements, by the order in which they are arranged, by the different demands they make, by the implicit and explicit ways in which it relates those demands, and even in the choices it offers students and the ways in which those choices are described. One test of a curriculum in this sense is precisely whether it can actually survive in its educational function a more or less complete change of teaching personnel. Actually, no curriculum can be entirely unaltered by such changes, but if one puts the question in another form (that is, Is it practically imaginable that a curriculum could survive such a change provided that the curricular function of its diverse elements were still understood where that was essential?) serious standards are being invoked. What is really being asked is whether curricular intent is in fact communicable and the functions of elements sufficiently discriminated so that alternatives can be intelligently chosen or made available. Another way of subjecting a curriculum to such a "thought-experiment" is to ask whether a student who had been educated in it could give an account of its functional structure without that account becoming a recounting of the influence exerted on him by the personalities of his teachers. However, perhaps the most basic and important strategic point to be made about the curriculum as a teaching device is the one made earlier, namely, that it must effectively provide, in powerfully functional relationships, effective engagement in intellectual activity and habitualizing reflection upon that engagement. (Another way, incidentally, of evaluating a curriculum is to ask how it functions in the education of those teachers who work in it; but we shall return to that problem later.)

These first two considerations are largely derived from the requirement that a liberal curriculum be reflective and ethogenic. A third consideration is derived from the requirement that it be systematic. Curricular architecture for a liberal education must begin with and work from some map or plan of the intellectual world, some assumptions as to its organization, and this plan must have two characteristics: it must be complete (exhaustive) and it must be a structure of activities or disciplines. (Indeed the image of a map or plan is potentially misleading, because it suggests a surface or area to be covered rather than a systematic interrelation of functions or activities.) Many of the difficulties of educational strategy derive from the nature of such unavoidable presuppositions. First, there are many of them; second, they are seldom explicitly well-articulated in the minds of those who function by their use all the time; third, some are more easily translated into actual curricular possibilities in a given set of circumstances than others; fourth, some are better than others—though this last consideration is probably less important in practice than the other problems they present. In the terms of the problem as we have set it for ourselves, this prerequisite can be translated once again into a question of the appropriate mode of exploiting the diversities which are present in the university. What are the significant diversities and how can they be represented in a curriculum by the choice of available or to-be-constructed elements? From this point of view a conception of the intellectual world is a reduction of the diversity we discussed earlier as presented in any actual instance, to manageable curricular shape. Without it one cannot have any way of asking intelligent questions about substitutability of elements or the use of talents (for example, in teachers, but also in students) which represent diverse modes of functioning within a given discipline or across disciplinary possibilities. In its ideal form, again, it would guarantee that all the significant kinds of diversity of enterprise were effectively represented—every curriculum would be a selection from the elements available, but all would be complete. This last point entails the assertion (which could in fact have been derived earlier from other considerations) that there is no such thing as *the* liberal curriculum—there are liberal curricula. But again this is a point to which we shall return.

While such a structure is a functional prerequisite of the design of a curriculum, it is not what is taught in or by the curriculum. A fourth consideration to be kept in mind by all who engage in this sort of strategic thinking is that the function of such a "map" or organization is heuristic, not substantive. That is, it is a way of ordering and focusing reflective thought and its materials in a search for disciplines, not itself the disciplines which are to be taught. In other words, it should serve as a device for ensuring that disciplinary questions and problems are systematically raised and discussed rather than as a set of answers to the questions and resolutions of the problems. This consideration is of special importance in relation to the form in which the problem of institutionalizing a liberal curriculum presents itself most directly—the problem of recruiting (initially and continuously) a faculty which can and will support the enterprise *as such*. ("As such" is important, since we have already indicated the sense in which much faculty energy can be used in a curriculum without the requirement that the practitioners themselves have any active insight into or devotion to the enterprise as a whole.) If what is required as a condition of adherence to the effort is some full-fledged acceptance of a given way of thinking about the structure of the intellectual world, serious limitations are immediately put upon the availabilities. But if a curricular plan is put forward as an organization not of solutions but of the places in which solutions can be effectively discussed, the possibilities of genuine adherence are greatly broadened. Earlier we mentioned the possibility that a curriculum of this sort might serve to educate the faculty as well as the students. It will do so in proportion as its organization functions as places of discussion. A search for disciplines may be organized and systematic without being dogmatic—that is, without being committed to emerging with a predetermined solution. In that search, faculty and students alike must share, no doubt in somewhat different roles. We have argued that curricula educate and teach, but it is obvious that some consideration must be given to the roles of teachers and students in a curriculum. To do so would be to consider teaching (and learning) in something like a more recognizable sense. What we should recognize from the present vantage point is that teachers function in relation to each other as well as in relation to students.

But before we turn to the problems of teaching in this sense, we may make two observations having to do with curricular construction which arise largely from the possibilities inherent in the notion of a systematic organization. Speaking very broadly (even schematically) there are two different directions along which systematization may be attempted. One may be described as distributive and the other as centralizing. The first proceeds by spreading out the places in which disciplines are to be sought and consequently usually confronts problems of integration or interrelation among them. This pattern is evident in many general education programs which begin by organizing the world into the humanities, the sciences, and the social sciences or some other similar scheme. Yet to the extent that these are constituted and ordered as disciplinary regions, each will tend to yield a universal discipline which can accommodate all data, subsume all inquiries, and, in effect, serve as a center for the intellectual world. The centralizing possibility would proceed by choosing some center in this sense and arranging the other centers around it. If carried out with sufficient thoroughness, each will arrive at the beginning point of the other, but the organizational possibilities each presents may be decisively different in actual circumstances. From the point of view of conventional academic thinking, curricula of the first sort looks like distribution requirements gone mad (or simply made systematic), and the others look like exotic, interdisciplinary majors or concentrations (or novel and perhaps even interesting subject matters).

Yet as different ways of organizing and sustaining a search for disciplines, they may be equally effective.

Two consequences of these possibilities should, however, be noted. First, each contains many different possibilities, all in principle, though not circumstantially. equally plausible. There is no magic in any one way of organizing the search except insofar as one can be made to function in certain circumstances in which another will fail to enlist interest and attract resources. Thus there are many liberal curricula, and there is no good reason why there should not be a multiplicity of them available at a given institution or in diverse institutions. Secondly, short of the set of circumstances in which each of these possibilities can be worked out fully, there are many opportunities for the introduction of the reflective moment into educational processes which, though not sustained and systematic, are nonetheless worthy of exploitation. It is necessary to keep reminding oneself that one is attempting to locate and to stabilize an activity and a function, and that that problem is rarely equivalent to founding an institution and never to routinizing a set of devices. It is true that we seek to institutionalize functions and activities, but that effort is as much represented in the constant search for opportunities within institutions which have diverse functions and habits as it is in their complete reorganization. And, in any case, no organization is completely stable. One way or another we are always building the wall, sometimes a bit here and a bit there, or, to change the figure to a less discouraging one, we are always reinventing the wheel, and then of course complaining that a four-wheeled chariot does not immediately emerge.

II

If we turn now to the problems of teaching, in the sense in which it can be found in the activities of individual minds engaged in the actual work of liberal education, we may observe that it has two recognizable dimensions. First, there are the lines of activity in which the individual teacher is placed—or places himself or herself—in relation to a curricular structure and enterprise and, through that relationship, in relation to the institution within which that enterprise is undertaken. This is primarily, but not exclusively, a relationship with fellow teachers and all the other continuing elements and resources of the institution. Secondly, there is the line of activity in which a teacher functions primarily in the work of directly engaging students in the activity which is liberally educative. This is primarily, though again not exclusively, a matter of what happens in classrooms, courses, and other so-called teaching situations. In considering them we might keep in mind the salutary reflection that unless one assumes that one is the curriculum and that the growth of one's mind is complete, both are bound to be activities not only of teaching but of learning.

The attentive reader will no doubt have observed that much of what has been said about the devising of strategies requires only a very simple translation to become an analysis of the kinds of functioning which will be required of teachers, curricular architects, curricular collaborators, and what for want of a better expression we may call curricular instrumentalities or "instrumentalists." Everything so far said about strategies and the conditions to be met in devising them could be restated as a guide to the decision-making processes in which we seek out resources, relate them functionally, and arrive at some judgment of their efficacy. In effect, the individual teacher may find here the form of a discussion, a form which should enable him to organize his own thinking so as simultaneously to keep the discussion focused on a complex problem and to make contributions to it. It is no accident that in the exposition of that form we occasionally had recourse to some of the commonplaces—the specific arguments, maxims, or slogans which continually recur in such a discussion—in order to illustrate its problems. Usually, of course, the commonplaces cited were those which have the character of derailing the discussion as a whole or, at least, indicating that those who make use of them are unable or unwilling to enter into further consideration of the problems of a liberal curriculum. Nor is it an accident that we argued for such a use of these resources for the organization of discussion as would make them heuristic rather than doctrinal. In terms of individual activity, this is to urge an attitude toward other participants in the discussion which amounts to assuming a certain sort of character in it—the character of a contributor, a collaborator, and a listener. In other words, it is to be hoped that what we outlined is a series of strategies which, as the structure of a discussion, is oriented toward the discovery and the solution of common problems among widely diverse minds—minds which incorporate all the diversities we have so often referred to. The teacher is in the first instance one who is sensitive to and constantly working with these diversities as they present themselves in the competences and attitudes of those with whom he works—fellow scholars (or teachers) and students alike. It might well be objected, however, that the problems one confronts as a partisan of liberal education are not—at least not in the first instance—those of carrying on a discussion of institutional resources in the light of the criteria of reflective, habituating, systematic, and teleological activity. Once the discussion has reached that point, one might say, the battle is really won. Short of that one encounters narrow-minded prejudice, simple and complex forms of ignorance, trained incompetence, institutional inertia, and passions invested in the service of other functions and other enterprises. In other words, one enters the realm of politics and rhetoric —both in the worst senses which those much-abused words can have. One cannot deny that any practical discussion (and institutionalizing is a practical activity) may never get beyond the stages which are political and rhetorical in these senses or may, at almost any moment, degenerate into them. But one should recognize that these are ineluctable features, in some degree, of every human collaborative enterprise, and that to describe the situation in these terms (as above) is to run the risks of a self-fulfilling prophecy; after all, for practical purposes, such a characterization is a prophecy of failure. There are prejudices, ignorances, laziness, incompetences, and partisan passions in the academic world as elsewhere, but what in one man is a prejudice may be in another a well-considered judgment; ignorance may be combined with genuine docility and intelligence; a trained incompetence is the other side of a competence which may be useful; institutional and personal inertia may be a reliability of performance which can be harnessed so long as it is not disturbed; passionate devotion may actually be an asset if some common ground of purpose and function can be discovered. It is true that there is a difference between the conditions under which others may be used without violence to their integrity and those under which they can be enlisted as active collaborators in an enterprise; but which option is required can only be determined in the effort itself, and very little can be concluded from initial reactions. The political and rhetorical habit of mind is not one in which the world of other agents and resources is divided *a priori* into those that are available and those that are not; rather, that is what political and rhetorical activity endeavors to discriminate in an actual situation. For practical purposes—that is, in order to be practical—one must always assume that the inability to get such a process beyond the stage in which the merits of options can-

not be effectively considered, or a degeneration of collaborative behavior into such a condition, are not the intrusion of politics and
rhetoric but failures on the part of the politicians and the rhetori-
cians; failures of those who seek to act together and ground that
action in communication.

Nevertheless, it may be of some use to attempt a characterization
of those minds which are practically unavailable as colleagues to
be enlisted in the service of liberal education, if only because they
may serve to characterize their opposites. First and simplest, there
are those who for one reason or another are simply incapable of
reflection. (It is always interesting to speculate as to why they are
that way or how they got that way, but it is not necessary, and it is
seldom helpful.) In general there are two forms of this disability.
There are those who simply cannot detach what they are doing intellectually from the materials with which they happen to be engaged. There are more or less extreme forms of this syndrome. For
some, not only is it the case that criticism is *literary* criticism, it may
even be the case that literary criticism is Homeric criticism. That is
what they do, and they can do nothing else. (The mysteries of this
position are amusingly and profoundly probed in Plato's *Ion,* but
it is useless to recommend that work to such people.) Such persons
may be useful, in a limited way, but one cannot discuss criticism
with them. Another form is more complex: there are persons of far
greater sophistication in the sense that they have a well-developed
view of the intellectual world, but for them this view is literally
that, that is, it is simply what one sees when one looks at that world
—it is a given, a fact like any other fact. While they may be vaguely
aware that there are other views, they regard these as aberrations
of perception, as simple errors, or as metaphysical mysteries which
any intelligent and rational man can safely ignore. They are far
harder to make use of.

More difficult to deal with, partly because they frequently offer
themselves as eager collaborators in any program of educational
change, are those who are afflicted with one or another perversion of
the teleological function and intent of liberal education. Everything
we said earlier about the forms which such perversions—disloca-
tions and reductions—take is doubly relevant here. General education, for example, has suffered grievously from those who think
that all problems of man and society can be resolved in a given
inquiry, a specific discipline, or even a given subject matter, as well
as from those who have remorselessly focused attention on certain

questions or issues of the day as the basis for organizing a curriculum. And in many ways worst of all, since they effectively dissolve any disciplinary structure, are those who substitute for thought some concern for lofty goods and the celebration of encounters with great minds, great traditions, or ancient or modern wisdom. It is too easy to identify these confusing figures as those who have a message, for very frequently there is no discernible or, at least, simple message—no "truth that will set you free." Many of them seem, rather, simply fascinated with certain questions which they proceed to worry, like puppies chewing on an old shoe, almost indefinitely. Decision would deprive them of an occupation. Others seem to wish always to arrive at some lofty point of view from which all time and existence take on the shape of irresolvable and tragically moving spectacle—a "darkling plain . . . where ignorant armies clash by night"—a spectacle to be contemplated with a kind of superior adolescent detachment compounded of weariness and a satisfying sense of having faced the worst, the attitude of one "sustain[ing] alone, a weary but unyielding Atlas, the world that his own ideals have fashioned despite the trampling march of unconscious power."[7] But perhaps it is, after all, useless to attempt these characterizations, for as Aristotle remarked, the principles of error are infinite.

It is therefore with some sense of relief that we may turn to the problems of teaching and the teacher, in the narrower sense of working with students in specific curricular functions. It has already been argued that there may be many types of teaching which may legitimately have a place in a liberal curriculum. But here we may confine ourselves to a kind without which it is difficult to see that such a curriculum would come alive at all—that form of teaching which consists in "directly engaging students in the activity which is liberally educative." Since we have already discussed that activity extensively, it is not hard to describe this function of teaching: teaching in this sense is *a shared process of reflective thought.* Such a process would have three essential moments. First, an engagement of minds in a process of thought must be accomplished in and through communication; second, the objects of thought and the processes in which they are to be explored must be sufficiently elaborated, again by means which offer some reason to believe that

7. Bertrand Russell, "A Free Man's Worship," *Mysticism and Logic* (London: Longmans, Green and Co., 1918), p. 57.

it is shared, so as to form a worthy object for reflection; third, the common attention must be turned to the process of thought, and its objects as functions of it, as itself something to be explored and thought about. The teacher in this situation is primarily an initiator and a leader, initiating the engagement, leading the inquiry, judging when the reflective moment is ripe for initiation. But it is important to note that all of these roles or actions are functions within a process in which all the participants are active. Students and teacher alike must be searching for engagement, thinking through and about something, and turning their attention to what they have been doing. In other words, the roles here are not active and passive, but rather different functions in a shared activity. And exchanging of roles is to be expected and encouraged as the participants advance along the road. With his usual unerring skill in such matters, Plato has Socrates quote a line from Homer as he begins an inquiry in the *Protagoras*.[8] The line is, "When two go together, one discerns before the other," but the whole passage from which this line is selected is interesting. The warrior Diomedes is urging that some attempt be made upon the camp of the sleeping Trojans—an enterprise of some peril. He is willing to "go it alone," but says, "If some other man were to go with me, there would be greater comfort and greater confidence. When two go together, one discerns before the other how profit may be had; whereas if one alone perceives anything, still his sight is shorter and his ingenuity limited."[9] Enterprises of thought are perilous in many senses, and their communicability is not merely a test of their validity but a resource in conducting them.

Nevertheless, from the point of view of the teacher in these situations, his first task is to secure a genuine engagement in a process and with an object. Since the object is defined in the process, it can only be in the most superficial sense that there can be an antecedent engagement with it. Much discussion of teaching is devoted to the devices by which students may be induced to engage in the enterprise of thinking about something. It will be observed that this problem is proportionately related to teaching in the sense we are now exploring as the political and rhetorical problems we discussed earlier are related to the initiation of a discussion of educational policy and curricular construction. Again, it is extremely

8. *Protagoras,* 348C–D.
9. *Iliad,* X, 222–26.

difficult to say anything about these problems in general. The very words which could be used to describe the attitudes or condition of students in the initial stages of teaching are indicative of the nature of the problem. Students (or classes) are eager, apathetic, hostile, politely skeptical, puzzled, confused, interested, intimidated, and so on. All of these are, whatever else they may be, emotional, or affective, states, they are complex functions of previous experience, competences and incompetences, expectations and simple inattention, and they have their concomitants on the side of the teacher. In other words, the process of search for engagement might be described as determining how one's self is to be organized or ordered to this shared activity. And since it is shared, there is a mutual definition of selves in the community which carries on the activity. If it is at all successful, there will be a felt sense of community, shared interest, shared success and failure, and mutuality of purpose which can be called, without strain, friendship. Once more we may have recourse to Plato. In the *Lysis,* after a long and inconclusive but absorbing series of attempts to say something defensible about friendship, Socrates says to his youthful coadjutors, "Today, Lysis and Menexenus, we have made ourselves ridiculous—I, an old man, and you. For these others here will go away and tell how we think we are friends of one another—for I count myself in with you—but what a friend is we have not been able to discover."[10] How one arouses and focuses interest, establishes confidence, and initiates an organized activity in such complex situations is hardly subject to easy analysis. (How does one "make friends"?) But perhaps one may make some useful points.

First, just as in the case of the rhetorical character of curricular discussion, it is extremely important to take note that one's devices and behavior cannot be separated from the end which one is attempting to achieve. It is entirely possible to produce, from an apathetic or even hostile group of students, a happy, hardworking, interested, excited class with high morale and a capacity to produce vivid testimonials to the merits of the course and to the superior pedagogical abilities of its teacher by engaging them in activities which are not activities of thought and reflection. It is not that such activities are necessarily wicked or useless; it is simply that they are different. Some of them are, it must be admitted, a bit difficult to defend. Students sometimes become very interested in the teacher,

10. *Lysis,* 223B.

and the class becomes an entertainment—somtimes a very subtle and elaborate entertainment, a work of art—but the activity involved is rather more "Let us make a play" than "Let us think about something." And, of course, to pursue the analogy, the *dramatis personae* may be enlarged to include the students too. Some of this is probably unavoidable in any teaching; what is perverse from the point of view of liberal education is the stabilization of this activity, rather than its employment for the purpose of initiating and stabilizing another.

Second, there is much discussion of teaching—and even of the larger problems of curricular construction—which runs in terms of identifying students' interests (and the related competences) and using them as a starting point from which to develop other interests, or to expand them so that they require a commitment to all intellectual activity. Such approaches are not without merit, but they require careful handling. (It should be noted that "interests" tend to have curricular consequences in the situations of choice and election which continue to recur in our curricular procedures. Students are frequently asked, for the purpose of such decisions, what they are "interested in," and they are used to evaluating available options by reference to their interests. Sometimes an apathetic or hostile attitude in a given class is a function of their feeling that they would not be there if they were allowed to consult their interests.) In the first place, there is the general objection—or problem—that liberal education is devoted not only to the exploration and development of objects of interest but also to their discovery. It is not so much a process of doing what you are interested in as it is a search for what there is to be interested in. Insofar as "interest" restricts attention, it may inhibit growth. Moreover, it is dangerous to assume (and this really makes the same point in a different way) that students' interests are given and easy to identify. A student may evince an interest in French or mathematics, but it is not easy to say what there is about those ambiguous objects which is in fact the object of his interest. Frequently, they may simply reflect the fact that it is in dealing with those subject matters that he found his brains put to work, and that his (or her) interest is really in using brains, rather than in learning French or developing mathematical skills. If this is what might be meant by enlarging interests to encompass the whole range of intellectual possibilities, it may be fruitful; but it is not obviously the easy way to go about the job. Finally, there may lurk in this way of thinking an assumption that somehow the processes of education may be painless if the student is imperceptibly led, simply by doing what he is good at and following his already aroused interests, into doing other things and arousing other interests. This is a recipe for avoiding reflection, and therefore, from the point of view of liberal education, simply counterproductive. One may seriously doubt that thinking can develop without those moments of radical puzzlement when what is in question is not simply the next step in some inquiry but the status of the inquiry itself. While these moments are not comfortable, they are potentially the most productive of an enhanced and refined purposiveness, even though in them objects dissolve, intention falters, and purposes not only seem to offer no guidance but are deprived of their status.

So far we have discussed the problems in terms which are universal enough almost to justify calling them *human* problems of teaching and learning. If we turn to those problems which might seem more particularly related to the kinds of cultural artifacts, in the form of human beings, we are likely to encounter in the institutions which we know and in which we have to work, we encounter again unavoidable problems of tendencies, trends, and assessment of importance. Much complaint is always forthcoming from college teachers about the competences and incompetences which entering students bring with them. Students cannot write grammatical sentences; students are not required to learn languages, or are encouraged to learn useless ones; students have weak backgrounds in mathematics, in science, in literature; students have never read a book, or they have read all the wrong ones; they know no history and they have hardly even heard of economics. But we might contend that the most serious problem about entering college students is not a product of their incompetence but of what in an important sense, they are good at. Or perhaps it would be better to say that the most serious problems are presented by what are, by the usual criteria, the best or among the best students. It is characteristic of such students that they have little difficulty in becoming engaged with any ordered inquiry which is set before them. In this sense they are docile. And they are extremely efficient in assimilating large bodies of highly organized information—that is, at mastering subject matters. But they are scarcely aware of the intellectual order which organizes the material; in fact, they are not conscious of themselves as engaged in inquiry or as reconstructing or reconstituting the results of inquiry. They are very good *learners,* in other words, but they have never, in an important sense, *thought* about anything. To recur to terms we employed earlier, their expectations are that they will be expected to master a body of material, and they expect to do so. These students quite naturally want to know what a course is about, what it covers, how far it may be expected to take them, and what they will know when they complete it. An image of such students—eager and efficient but somehow out of their accustomed element—is contained in a story told by Philipp Frank of his experience in teaching the philosophy of science at Harvard. After about the third or fourth lecture, he would be waited upon by a group of students, clutching the notebooks in which as yet they had found nothing to record, asking (politely, of course, in those days of good manners) "Professor Frank, could you give us some idea of the material you intend to cover in this course." And he would reply, with obvious relish, "I do not cover material; I am not a materialist."

Such an experience is, for students, a frustrating one. If material is not covered, what does one do and what is one supposed to learn? Such violations of habitual expectations can be silently or even violently resisted, and the process of creating new expectations can be painful and exhausting. In effect a liberal arts college or a curriculum or a course ought to have a sign on it for the benefit of students: "Here there is nothing to learn; there are only things to think about." (Incidentally, it is important to recognize that this should be a *curricular* message; one of the powerful senses in which a curriculum teaches is precisely in the way it reshapes expectations to this end.) But there are difficulties with this idea. In the first place it is, in this form, inaccurate (though provocative). It would be more accurate to say, "Here there is nothing to learn except as something to think about," or (more accurate and more encouraging), "Here you will learn much because there are so many interesting things to think about." But one could go on reshaping the slogan indefinitely and never say anything more to the sort of student just described than that he may be moving into a puzzling situation, for *ex hypothesi* the distinction in all forms of the slogan is one which he cannot relate to his experience of teaching and learning and to his own activity as a student. The slogan, if literally used, would simply say to him, "Maybe you can expect something unprecedented." Such slogans are not without utility, though they may intimidate as well as attract, but unless a curriculum and a course can realize the expectations which the formula prophecies, by effecting an engagement of the student in an unaccustomed activity, the terms employed will remain meaningless to him. So we return to where we started, to the problem of ways of initiating and sustaining thinking in this sense.

Another characteristic of many very good students, as they are presently identified by our educational institutions, is that they are "highly motivated." One of the most persistent forms of motivation has to do with expectations in a somewhat different sense. I remarked earlier that studies of how knowledge enriches life frequently discover that it does not. One simple example of that fact is the current "research" which tends to throw grave doubt on the importance and utility of a college education, or of education beyond high school, which is not clearly oriented vocationally. (Liberal arts degrees, in that amorphous sense discussed earlier, tend to be particularly vulnerable in these researches.) It is easy to dismiss this sort of concern by stigmatizing it as vulgar: "Knowledge does not necessarily enrich you, therefore it does not enrich life." But such a concern and such a motivation are in fact wider in scope and more pervasive among students (and teachers, who, after all, were once students and have pursued their specialities with some consequence for their lives) than such "vulgar" reductions might suggest. In a way, we have already considered these problems of motivation when discussing the possibilities of building a curriculum or a course around student interests, but students are motivated not only by interests but also by a nagging sense that their interests and their educations ought to emerge in careers. Indeed, they frequently think of themselves as sacrificing interests in the service of a career. The tendency to think of education as an investment which ought to pay off, the natural ambitions of the young and talented, and the powerful rhetoric of service to the community which, as we have seen, is not a new phenomenon in American education, but has been part of institutional ideology and has expressed itself in curricular thinking from the beginning, not only operate to produce external pressures on students (particularly the better ones) from parents and peers, but enter powerfully into their own assumptions about what they are doing and the choices they must make in doing it. Students have a genuine concern for where they are going, and they tend to think of that in terms of what they will be *doing,* not merely in the next six months but in the indefinite future, and the shape which doing takes in that extension is the shape of a career, an occupation, an identifiable contribution to security and happiness in activity which can be plausibly projected to develop along some normal pattern of expectation.

It is not necessarily the case that such a career is thought of primarily in terms of job opportunities and their relative remunerations. Robert Hutchins used to tell a story about, I believe, Jowett, who was once asked by an eager student, no doubt "highly motivated," "What is the use of Greek?" To which the Master replied, "Not only is it the immediate language of the Holy Spirit, but it leads to positions of great honor and emolument." Mr. Hutchins would then point out that nowadays the study of Greek leads to positions only in the teaching of Greek, adding, "While these are of great honor, they are not of great emolument." Greek may not yet have been affected, but there is serious consideration being given to the possibility of restricting the number of persons who will be allowed to achieve advanced degrees in certain fields precisely because there are so few positions available. One may debate the appropriateness of such a move with respect to advanced degrees, but the attitude implicit in the question and the tensions visible in the answer are present in the minds of students and teachers long before there is any question of the choice of a Ph.D. program. It is worth giving some thought to what questions may be in the minds of students when they ask questions which *can* be interpreted as simply reducing the problem to "What kind of job can I get, or for what further job-training will this prepare me, and what are the chances for increasing status and salary along the line I may see myself pursuing?" If we interpret the question as really asking what sort of life am I making for myself, and therefore (to use a Deweyan formula) "What sort of self is in the making?" it will seem at once a less vulgar, more reasonable, and also a more difficult question, because it may seem to deserve an answer. F. H. Bradley, discussing a similar question ("Why should I be moral?") asserted that if the question is interpreted as " 'What is the use' of goodness, or beauty, or truth . . . there is but one fitting answer from the friends of science, of art, or religion and virtue, 'We do not know, and we do not care.' "[11] And as a way of inducing reflection on the relevance and status of the question, an answer of that sort has a certain effectiveness when students ask, as they frequently do, what can

11. F. H. Bradley, *Ethical Studies* (Oxford: Oxford University Press, 1927), p. 63.

be done with an education in a liberal curriculum, or, in effect, where does this point me with respect to a career? At least it has the merit of emphasizing in a negative form what is an important truth, namely, that no specific occupational direction is or ought to be entailed by such a curriculum. Have we not argued again and again that such an education will confer "control over intellectual powers" which may then be exerted "in *any* special direction?" But what is the positive form of the answer to the question? "You will gain control over your intellectual powers"? Again the answer may not seem persuasive, not because it is vague, but because there is no identifiable reference for it in the experience of those who ask the question. For one who has achieved some control over his thinking processes, it is not vague; it is a precise and rich formula. One is tempted to answer the question somewhat wryly by saying that a liberal education is just something to "live with," but whatever form the answer takes it should emphasize two things: first, what *may* emerge (and one cannot promise that it *will* emerge) is a quality of life, of living, of activities; and second, this quality will be manifest in *everything* one does, not only in some exotic occupations or curious objects of interest outside of one's occupation or career. Otherwise, liberal education is again placed among the occupations of leisure, in the sense in which that is opposed to the serious business of life. What after all is more serious than the sort of person one may become?

But in the long run the answer to the question must be found in the engagement in activities which disclose new objects of interest as the fruits of new activities and confer an enhanced sense of control over one's activities in a novel purposefulness. Thus, we must return again to problems of teaching "technique," that is, how to effect this engagement, in a narrower sense. It is sometimes thought, and not without reason, that there are certain devices or procedures of teaching which are more appropriate than others for the purposes of a liberal education. The essential requirements, after all, of any teaching of this sort are relatively easy to state. After initial engagement, student and teacher must undertake an activity of intellectual construction or reconstruction, and then this activity and the construct which is its product or object must themselves become the object of attention *as such*. The whole process must then be repeated, both in the interest of clarifying constructive or reconstructive activity and ultimately in testing out the possibilities of changes in that activity—that is, of observing what difference it makes as one goes at it differently. Some procedures of teaching do seem more appropriate to these functions than others. In particular, it is urged that something called "teaching by discussion," or "teaching by asking questions," or the "Socratic method" have special powers for initiating and sustaining this process. And it is not hard to see why this might be so. We have said that teaching is a shared process of reflective thought. Discussions seems to incorporate sharing and communicating in a far more direct way than do lecturing and reciting (a word hardly ever used any more, but an activity which remains pervasive). And since we are concerned with activities, questioning seems to be an appropriate device not only because it requires the give-and-take which communicating directly implicates, but because it seems to require from the beginning that the student do something, that he participate actively. And, as we all know, Socrates, knowing nothing himself, worked entirely by eliciting what others knew and submitting it to test by questioning. And there is much to be said for these devices in these terms. One may observe, for instance, with respect to the problems of student expectations and learning which we have just been exploring, that for a student with many "normal" expectations, it is a considerable shock to enter a class in which everything begins with a question, for it seems to say, or may seem to say, "I have nothing to tell you, nothing to teach; but you are going to *do* something here." Elaborate revisions of expectations may be consequent upon that shock. (To be sure, such a student may also drop the course or remain silently puzzled throughout it.)

But there are serious objections to an easy acceptance of these formulae for successful teaching. One way of stating these objections is to suggest the limitations of the formula. First, discussion too easily turns into the simple requirement that everybody participate or that everybody express his or her opinion. There are certain processes of thought in which the disciplined expression of opinion is useful, but expression for the sake of expression or in aid of a sense of participating can rapidly degenerate teaching into the encouragement of a bull session or debate. These activities may be exciting and satisfying (at least for those who triumph), but they have little to do with intellectual construction. Secondly, if by questioning we mean simply employing the interrogative mode (or mood), very little has been specified. It is extremely difficult to frame and to ask the kinds of questions which initiate processes of thought and reflection. Questions may be, in effect, catechetical (that is, requiring recitation) or provocative (requiring expression), or they may be dialectical (requiring thought), though one hesitates to use this last word because of its more grandiose associations. Further, if one in fact consults the Platonic (or even the Socratic dialogues) one finds a bewildering array of teaching and learning situations and rapidly loses the simple conviction that anything much has been said by stating that Socrates taught by asking questions. One will find in them long lectures (as in the *Protagoras* or the *Phaedrus*), minilectures (as in the famous passage expounding the doctrine of reminiscence in the *Meno*), and a striking variety of effective and ineffective constructive efforts in significantly different question-and-answer forms. All of these might be easily subsumed under the headings of "dialogues within speeches" or "speeches within dialogues," but all that tells us is that we have not found out what a dialogue or a speech may effectively, pedagogically be.

The fact is that all these devices may be appropriate in the activity we are attempting to structure, provided that we recognize the complexity of its moments or "phases." Catechetical questions such as those which in effect ask "What is said on p. 62" or "What is Boyle's law?" (where the answer expected is simply the accurate recitation of the formula rather than some such answer as a proportion or a principle of physics) may be perfectly appropriate as a way of assembling material for constructive activity or pointing to some phase in its progress. Lectures may be ways of asking questions, of setting forth constructions which can form the basis of powerful reflective questions, or (given practiced lecturers and listeners) they may be shared processes of reflective thought. What a lecture or a discussion or Socratic teaching may be is different in each of these functional phases, and no format can take the place of recognizing these differences and the sensitivity to them which issues in a judgment as to what is required at a given moment in the development of a discussion or a dialogue. In large part, perhaps, our difficulties here stem from taking too short a view of what is going on. The unit of teaching or dialogue may be considered for some purposes to be a class session or a lecture hour; for others it may be fruitful to find a unit in a given series of such hours or classes; for another the course is the dialogue; and, as we have already argued, in another and important sense the curriculum is the instructional unit within which all the phases of intellectual activity can be found. Here again we may take a lesson from Plato. How long would it take to carry on the conversation which is the *Republic* (a conversation in which there are, incidentally, debates, catechetical moments, long speeches—some of them stories—and so on)? Could it be done in a ten weeks course? Is it a curriculum?

A treatise on teaching in a liberal curriculum—and there is no intention of elaborating one here—could do worse than base itself upon the Platonic dialogues, treating them not as embodying a particular intellectual or philosophic method or a special set of metaphysical assumptions, but as exemplary of the disciplined use of a variety of devices not only responsive to different sorts of pedagogical situations but creative of new ones in the sequence of thought, and of the tactful discrimination of the moments of the process of thought which require different devices and different questions. Above all, perhaps, such an investigation would be an education in the art of framing fruitful pedagogical questions, questions which take into account the answerer as his mind is related to whatever phase the inquiry may have reached, the kind of inquiry it is, the relation of questioner to both phase of inquiry and to answerer, and the choice of those moments which are moments of radical change of direction of attention. Were I to attempt to anticipate the conclusion of such a treatise so far as it could be translated into a characterization of the teacher, I would say two things. First, a teacher is one who can frame questions which arouse an interest in and focus attention upon functionings of principles, and second, a teacher is one who knows where the process of thought has been and is going, not in the sense that he knows what the result will be, but in the sense that he knows what the moments of such an activity are and in which of them, as an ordered and functional sequence, the process is at a given moment. In support of these grand and certainly somewhat mysterious assertions one may cite two authorities.

To take the latter point first, we may note that Socrates says in the *Republic* that a philosopher must have a good memory.[12] At first sight this seems to contradict what he says about himself on other occasions and the whole point of the processes of inquiry and discovery which the dialogues represent. But we may also remember that Aristotle records that Plato was always asking, "Are we on our way to or from what is first?"[13] That ability to locate oneself

---

12. *Republic*, VII, 535B–C.
13. *Nicomachean Ethics*, I, 4 (1095a 32–34).

in the movement of thought, to keep and have in mind its actual and projected career, the direction which its past projects and its future may realize might well be said to require a good memory. Without it, inquiry and thought could be little else than what Kant picturesquely describes as "poking around"—*Herumtappen*. And it is Kant who is our other authority, though the point to be made is implicit in Aristotle's reference to Plato's habits. In a characteristically meaty and very contextually pointed discussion of teaching devices Kant, distinguishing two kinds of erotematic or teaching-by-questioning situations, differentiates them by whether the questions are addressed to the memory or to the reason of the student.[14] "Reason" is for Kant no vague word: reason is that intellectual function which is directed to the construction of inferential relationships; in other words, since such a construction depends upon differentiating what is inferrable or consequent from that from which it is inferred or on which it is consequent, that which is more basic and from which one can begin, reason is the capacity to organize thought by reference to principles. No wonder Plato was always asking which way we are going.

These authorities may not be overwhelming, but they may at least function suggestively, or, we might better say, heuristically— that is, they may serve to initiate organized processes of thought about teaching. In pursuit of a final point, more of what Kant has to say is relevant.

[I]f one seeks to direct one's questions to someone's reason, then the procedure cannot be other than *dialogical* [*dialogisch*], that is, it must be accomplished in a procedure wherein teacher and student reciprocally ask and answer. The teacher guides the student's process of thought by questions in the sense that he merely develops the potentiality for definite thoughts in the student by setting cases before him (that is, he is the midwife of the student's thoughts); the student, who in the process becomes aware that he himself is capable of thought, demands by *his* questions (about obscurities or doubts directed at the propositions advanced) that the teacher—according to the maxim "by teaching we learn" [*docendo discimus*]—himself learns what is required to ask good questions [*wie er gut fragen müsse*].

It is obvious, as the context would also suggest, that Kant is here

14. *Metaphysische Anfangsgründe der Tugendlehre*, Prussian Academy Edition, *Werke*, vol. 6 (Berlin, 1907) p. 478.

addressing himself to problems of a much earlier stage of intellectual development than those with which we might think we are
concerned, but intriguing points emerge even in this limited context. First, the "dialogical" (a better word than "dialectical," since
it avoids some confusing associations) procedure is inherently a
reciprocal process. Second, in this process the student becomes
aware of (*wird inne*) his own abilities, his own capacities. Third,
what the teacher learns is how to ask good questions. If we recognize the close connection, if one is concerned with a process of
reflective inquiry, between good pedagogical questions and questions that are good in the sense of initiating and sustaining significant inquiry, we may put together these three points into a pro-
jection of the end of the process of teaching. An end would be
reached when the student, fully aware of his powers and their structured relation to the asking of good questions in both senses, would
be able to exchange roles with the teacher so that either would be
leader or coadjutor indifferently, or only as determined by their
relation at a given moment to an actual process of thought. "When
two go together, one discerns before the other how profit may be
had; whereas if one alone perceives anything, still his sight is shorter
and his ingenuity limited." In other words, the ultimate aim of the
teacher is to disappear *as such*. But in this sort of educational process he will disappear not with the words "I have taught you everything I know" but rather with "You can do it as well as I," or, quite
simply, "You're on your own now," not in the sense in which that
phrase might suggest abandonment but in the way in which is recog-
nizes maturity. But preferable to either is something as simple as
"Where do *we* go from here?"

Index